Imprisoned By The Past...
The Caged Bird Still Sings

Chantiele "Shae Mone" Brazzell

ABOUT THE AUTHOR

Brazzell, a native Detroiter, is not only a phenomenal singer, chef, philanthropist but a literary expressionist. Chantiele believes that laughter and all forms of art are the best medicine. That's why she authentically uses every gift that has been bestowed upon her to entertain, motivate, heal, inspire and be an overall blessing to others.

With an early start in music, she began like most in the church choir. "Shae Mone'" as she is affectionately known to fans and friends alike, made a name for herself with bookings across Metro Detroit to Atlanta, GA. Brazzell's strong vocals garnered her work with the artist, Michael Powell of Chapter 8 as well as other musical contributions with local and nationally known artists.

Outside of her musical ingenuity, Chantiele studied culinary arts at Dorsey Culinary Institute, where she earned a certification. A health care provider and educated Journalist, it is evident that Brazzell is multi-talented, gifted and a heart for service.

DEDICATION

This book is dedicated to my late mother…

Regina (Brazzell) Hardin.

I love and miss you my angel.

Prologue

This was now the second time that I'd felt cast to the side by the woman that I so desperately wanted to be with. I knew I wasn't perfect, by any means, but damn… did I deserve this? I didn't know what to do but run away. I felt unwanted and unwelcomed. I remembered feeling so abandoned when my mother would come home on her drunken rants and decide to put me out. Not before she fought me like I was someone on the street, though. I would find myself walking, sometimes at 3 or 4 in the morning, alone, aimlessly in the dark. Before long, I just started leaving on my own. Occasionally, my honorary Godparents would let me sleep over at their house. They were like family to me. Their daughter, Emily, and I were best friends in middle and high school, and they took me in and picked up where my parents lacked. Godfather or Paw as I affectionately called him, had connections in the music industry. He took me under his wing and started managing my early music career. He got me all kinds of studio and showed work when I was just a teenager. He believed in me and my talent, but aside from that, he cared about me like one of his kids. I thought of him much like a dad as well. He was kind but protective, the way I felt a dad should be.

I remember staying the night at their house and my sperm donor calling there to talk to me. I was stunned at what he had to say. He accused me of sleeping with my 40-year-old Godfather. I was floored and hurt. I couldn't understand at the time how he could even fathom such a thought about his fourteen-year-old daughter. But then this was the same man who had performed sexual acts with me, his daughter. Paw was always straight up with all of us kids, but never inappropriate. He loved us all like his own. Maybe my dad was just jealous of our relationship. I was appalled that HE would always say the foul shit to me. He'd say explicit, inappropriate things that a father should never say to his child. I remember coming home from school one day when I was in fifth grade. Some rude boy had said to me and another girl that he wanted us to "suck him up." I ran home to my father upset and crying. I told him what that ingrate said to me, and he erupted in laughter. He said "don't worry. One day you'll step up to the "mic" and give your BEST performance." I didn't even know what that meant at the time, but the mere fact that he'd laughed when I was so hurt was enough to break me down. I cried incessantly. I was shocked at his reaction. I wanted him to go to that school and snap that boy's neck! I wanted him to defend and protect me. Instead, he broke my heart before any nigga had a chance to. Maybe that's why I never really attached feelings to any man. In my mind, none of them could ever be trusted.

Chapter 1

I'm sitting on my couch in the dark with the window cracked enjoying the breeze on this autumn day. It's sixty degrees outside, and that's exceptional for an October day in the city of Detroit. I was born and raised in the concrete jungle. I wouldn't call myself a street person, but I know my way around the streets. As I sit in my apartment and look around, I know that I am truly blessed. My rent and bills are paid, and I have money in the bank. However, this hasn't always been the case. I have been asked by many people, "Why do you sit in the dark?" My answer is still the same, "Because I do my best damn thinking in the dark!" I continued to sit and allow my mind to drift away, back to a not so happy time...

When I reflect back upon my childhood some of the memories make me smile and others I am truly saddened by. There are times I pray to forget some of my some of the childhood memories. I did have happy moments growing up, but they were overshadowed by the sad times. My mother worked hard to provide, but due to my youthfulness, I couldn't appreciate just how hard she worked to support the two of us. It seemed to me, in my youth that I came last in her life. Although my mother worked hard to keep a roof over our head, she had a weakness: (her man), because of that I often felt neglected and unloved. At that time, she was dating a man named Carlos. My mother considered him a catch because he was a decent looking man with a job. I don't recall when she met him, but I didn't like him. For as far back as I can remember she'd had a predictable pattern. Her career always came first; her romantic relationships; and I always pulled up the rear. I felt as if I had no place in her life, and that hurt me. My mother and I did not have a loving mother-daughter relationship.

Although, my mother fell short in a lot of areas my paternal grandmother picked up the slack. She was the total opposite of my mother. My mother could be cold and abrasive, but my grandmother was kind and loving. My grandmother always made me feel loved. As a child, I spent most weekends and holidays at her house. Her home was my haven. One of the things I miss most is waking up to beautiful smells of her baking and cooking dinner for the holidays. My grandmother could cook anything, and she passed that gift onto me. My grandmother passed away when I was ten years old, and the one beautiful constant thing I had in my life was gone. I was devastated. When my grandmother passed away, suddenly, the haven I knew no longer existed. Until then, I'd been able to escape the unstable life my mother had built for us. After the passing of my grandmother, my mother treated me with disdain. It seemed that, with my grandmother gone, my mother was now forced to bear the responsibility of parenting me on her own and she resented me for it. It was then that our relationship became increasingly turbulent.

Shortly, after the passing of my grandmother, my mother began a not so subtle pattern. Every day when I'd come home from school, she'd say "I'm going to the store." She'd stay "gone to the store" from three in the afternoon until anywhere from three to six in the morning. At this time, I wanted to bond with my mother with the recent death of my grandmother, but, she was rarely physically or emotionally available. This behavior went on for months. Every night, I found myself frantically calling family members and friends, asking anxiously "Have you seen my mother?" The answer was always "no." Then, after having had no sleep, I'd begin to get myself ready for school the following morning, and like clockwork, my mother would come strolling in like shit was normal. She didn't give a fuck that her behavior was traumatizing her ten-year-old child. One morning, after one of her disappearing acts, I was awakened by a loud argument between her and Carlos. He wanted to know where she had been.

"You fucking think I'm stupid?! You think I don't know you've been out all-night smoking that shit?" He asked angrily.

"What shit? What the fuck are you talking about, Carlos?" She asked, defensively.

"You're on crack! You know what the fuck I'm talking about, Gene! You a fucking drug addict!" He retorted even louder. I didn't understand what was going on. This was too much for my young mind to comprehend. I had never looked at my mother as a crack addict. That was the first time I ever thought of my mother in that capacity. I'd seen how drugs affected other people and how it made them act, but my mother kept a good job, and nothing in our house ever went missing. Now, her behavior in the last months all made sense. However, I lived in denial, for a long time after that. I just really couldn't imagine categorizing my mother as a neighborhood crack head, doing anything for their next high. I didn't view her that way, but Carlos did. In fact, any time he had a chance, he verbalized his disgust of her, and there were times I would be in earshot of the awful things he would say. All I wanted and needed was for her to be a mother, but she was incapable of doing that. With the recent loss of my grandmother and now discovering my mother was using drugs I was devastated and had no one to turn to.

For a child their home is where they go to find solace; but not for me. I wish I could honestly say that my mother's drug use was the only horrific thing going on in my life at that time. It wasn't. My mother was abusing drugs, but it was me she harmed the most. Verbally, physically and emotionally. My memory fails me as to what age I was when it began, maybe that's' for the best. I still don't know if the abuse came at the expense of the drugs or the mere fact that she just didn't want to be a mother. A mother to me, especially. Some of the beatings I can vividly recall, and others return like tiny fragments. My mother would hit me with anything in reach. There wasn't anything in particular that I was doing to trigger these beating, other than being her child. My mother once held me down and slammed my head into the floor repeatedly. I thought I was going to die. The straps and cords were the worst though. As I close my eyes, I can feel the straps tearing into my flesh. Once, the bruises on my legs and back were so severe that they bled for days before a scab grew over them. Changing for gym class gave me the same trembling feeling as the beatings. I was embarrassed, terrified of the consequences I'd face if anyone saw the bruises; old and new. Our family secrets would be exposed all over the school, and that wouldn't turn out good for me in the end. "How did I become so unlucky in life?"

Shit, at one point I was seriously confused about my name. She was more comfortable with names like little bitch, stupid motherfucker, and the "classic" fat ass. I guess you can say that the most important lesson my mother wanted to teach to me was that, "I wasn't worthy of being loved authentically or unconditionally." She validated her hatred for me by looking me dead in the face and telling me she hoped I died. The older I became the beatings became more frequent and severe.

I remembered how my mother would stumble in drunk or high at two or three a.m. and start fights with me. Whatever she could get her hands – she would hit me with it. Phone cords, hangers, shoes, you name it. One day, everything came to a head. My mother lost control, and she was hitting me with a rubber cord. She stopped beating me and picked up the massive glass pane from the coffee table I'd taken refuge behind. She swung it, and it seemed to shatter in mid-air. A chard came down and sliced open the top of my foot. I could see a slight sense of worry in my mother's eyes as she glanced down to take a quick look but never ceasing to stop striking me. The top of my foot split open and bled profusely. I'm sure I needed stitches, but she refused to take me to the hospital. I soaked towel after towel trying to stop the bleeding and finally ended up bandaging myself with a torn rag and masking tape from the kitchen junk drawer. Aside from her physically attacking me like I was a stranger, I was also subject to horrible names like bitch, hoe, tramp, slut, etc. I was always accused of not only being sexually active but sleeping around. As far as my mother was concerned, I was an eleven-year-old hooker. The discharge in my underwear was a direct result of me being a "nasty, fast hoe" in her opinion. Ironically, my mother's words and her low idea of me hurt far more than any beating. If this was the woman who had given me life, and this is what she thought of me, then it must be true. Who would know better what they created, better than the Creator themselves? At some point, I stopped crying and accepted my fate. I became desensitized to her verbal cutting, or so I thought.

Her abuse left me feeling emotionally broken. She couldn't possibly love me and hurt me this way. The friction between my mother and I only escalated throughout my adolescence. The beatings with straps and cords turned into knock-down, drag-out brawls. I grew tired of the feeling worthless. I felt a profound emptiness, and my heart ached every time she beat me or called me a name. It was like she enjoyed demeaning me. I'm sure she had her reasons for directing all of her frustrations towards me. Carlos witnessed but would never intervene.

My mother and Carlos had been together for so long that I can't remember him not being there. My mother was at her best when she was serving her man. I can remember being the basis of a lot of arguments between my mother and Carlos. Although my mother was very mean to me, she never allowed him to be. He wasn't allowed to reprimand or chastise me in any way. This was strange because my mother was always so quick to let relatives and even teachers to discipline me, which made me angry. She treated him like a king and paid little attention to me, and I hated him for it. I blamed him for our broken mother/daughter relationship. I would purposely do things to anger him. I thought if I were mean enough he'd pack his shit and leave. I understood that he wasn't the root of our problem. I just needed something or someone to blame for the lack of love and attention I so desperately needed from my mother. I desired a better relationship with my her, but she only gave me negative attention.

I remembered being young and all of the physical punishment I'd suffered at the hands of them both. My father, who after having done sexual acts with me when I was too young even to verbalize what was going on, had traded in that behavior for beatings. It didn't take much to set him off, and his recourse would always be physical, even though the mere sound of his voice terrified me. I remembered wetting the bed repeatedly as a child and every time being whipped with a belt, along with verbal taunting and humiliation. It seemed the more I cried, the more he lashed out. Maybe he liked hearing me cry or watching me suffer.

Chapter 2

I knew I had to get away from my mother, but I had no one to confide in. After the death of my grandmother, I was truly alone. My father was living but never played an active role in my life. The thought of him, to this day, disgusts me. When I visited my grandmother's home I, also, visited him, because he lived there. He didn't have the mental capacity to take on the responsibility of raising a child. Hell, he lived with my grandmother well into his thirties, and frankly, he needed to be parented. He was a fucking deadbeat. Ironically, Carlos wasn't allowed to even yell at me, but my father did. He was physical; emotionally, and sexually abusive. The sexual abuse took place when I was too young to verbalize it, but the memories ring true even today. At the time, I was angry and blamed my mother for not preventing this for as long as I can remember. I often wondered why she didn't know that her child was being victimized. Could she not see the signs? Did she not care? Was she so wrapped up in her little world that she didn't see the red flags? I'd later come to realize that maybe this was a thing that was not so foreign to her after all. Perhaps this was her idea of normality, because, probably, she'd been a victim herself.

When my grandmother passed my father inherited her once immaculate home. It was heartbreaking to watch all of the hard work my grandmother put into her home be slowly destroyed by someone so undeserving. He moved his girlfriend and her children in. They were not married but I considered them family. I gained two sisters, Nyema and Asia and a brother named Montrell. Asia, who was a month younger than me, as well as Montrell had learning disabilities. Asia's speech impairments were a little more severe than Montrell's, which is the reason she had to attend schools for impaired children. If you ask me, I'd say it was because their mother wasn't the sharpest knife in the drawer herself. Although an adulterer, who began an affair with my father while still married; I was empathic to Roseanne. She was obese; not very intelligent; which made her lack of self-esteem painfully apparent. It also made her the target of my father's rage. He was very demeaning and at times dehumanizing towards this woman who loved the ground he walked on. She catered to his every need, cooking, cleaning, bathing him, you name it. Yet, Roseanne wasn't even allowed to sleep in the same bed or room with him. In retrospect, my father was a bully, and no one was exempt from his abuse, not me and probably not Roseanne. He wasn't just abusive, he was a male chauvinistic pig who wouldn't even address Roseanne in public as his woman. She never said anything, never hit back, never left - not also when his rage spilled out and onto her children. Children that were not biologically his. I can't measure if my father was worse to me, her or her children. Nyema, Asia and Montrell were so afraid of my father that they would urinate in buckets or bottles to avoid the risk of waking up my father going to the bathroom. It seemed to be a pattern with the women in my life - I could see it in her eyes sometimes, Roseanne was terrified, had low self-esteem and would never stand up to my father. Not for herself, not for her children and surely not me. Roseanne taught me that

My childhood memories of my father may equally match those of my mother. However, I can thank dear old dad for passing on to me his genetic gift of song. Out of off the bullshit he did to me and to those I loved - I get chills whenever I open up my mouth and the melody of music leaves my soul and echoes through whatever room I'm in. Now that is all my father, the part of him I can love and appreciate.

No matter what was happening in my life performing in front of an audience gave me a sense of freedom. It didn't matter who or what the audience consisted of when I was singing it felt as if I was escaping the whole world; a euphoria almost. When I was about eleven, shortly after my grandma passed, my father began setting up singing gigs, mostly weddings. Occasionally, the couple to be married would request that I sing something solo, but most of the time I would sing a duet with my father. If he was nothing else, he was a dynamic singer. He could croon and woo women with his smooth angelic tone. Not to mention he had a vast knowledge of music.

One Saturday during the summer of *June 1991*, we were hired to sing at a wedding. The couple was friends of the organist at our church, who often referred us to singing gigs. He, also, coached me vocally and taught me piano until I became bored. This particular gig paid sixty dollars each. I felt like that was big money for an eleven-year-old at the time. After the wedding, we were paid and headed home. I was excited and carefully planning how to spend my money. I had sung before, but this was my first time as a hired vocalist. I got home to find my stepsisters out on the porch playing. It was summer and warm outside, so there was plenty of activity on our block. Kids were riding their bikes up and down the street while cliques of boys and girls congregated in front of the houses and on porches. There was always the sweet, smoky aroma of barbeque being prepared at any number of backyards in our close-knit community. Everyone knew each other, and our block was much like one big family. I asked Asia if she wanted to walk to the store with me. We didn't have to ask permission, as neither parent cared about our whereabouts so long as we were out of their faces until the street lights came on. She happily agreed, and we headed off to the store on nearby Fenkell Avenue.

"Hey! Wait for me" Nyema called." She ran to catch up to us. She always wanted to tag along. She was the baby, and strangely, she was closer to me than her sister. I always thought it was because she and I shared the same birthday, but perhaps there were other reasons.

As we entered the store, I told the girls they could pick out what they wanted for my treat. We left the store, happy with our selections, and headed back toward the house. On the way, we passed a crowd of teenaged boys shooting dice on the corner. One of them, a boy I liked, spoke to me and winked. I chatted back and smiled. He was a tall caramel colored boy older than me, just how I wanted them. His name was Devaughn, and he'd seemed to take a liking to me. We'd exchange a few words and a wink or two in passing. I was interested in boys, but not sexually. Most of the boys in our neighborhood were sexually active and would always try to get us girls in a position to go further than just kissing. Some of the girls would, but I wasn't one of them. I was mature for my age, both physically and mentally. I guess this transcended in my social being. A lot of the adults would say I was "fast" because I was developing early, and I wasn't shy around boys like most girls my age. Truthfully, I wasn't sexually active. I just wasn't easily intimidated when it came to boys. We returned home to find the front door shut and the curtains drawn. We didn't think much of it as my father was mostly a recluse, only showing his face when certain friends would come around or send us to store runs or other errands. We settled down on the porch to enjoy our snacks when my father came to the door and told me to come in. I did so and was a little concerned at what I saw. He was dressed in a t-shirt and boxer shorts and beat up house shoes and was sweating as if he'd just sprinted to the corner and back. He said, "let me borrow ten dollars I'll pay you back on the first." Without hesitation, I did what I was asked and handed over the ten dollars from my pocket, leaving me with forty-five and some change from the money I'd earned earlier that day. "Thank you, baby girl," he said. Don't worry. He assured me he would pay me back. I went back out onto the porch, but not before my father ran past me and across the street. My stepsisters and I talked and played, staying close to the house. About twenty minutes later, my father emerged from the house across the street where all the known dope boys hung out, still sweating like a slave. He approached the porch and once again asked me if he could "borrow ten dollars." I agreed, not wanting to disappoint him. He turned on his heels before the money was in his hands right and sprinted across the street to the same house. He repeated that pattern until I was down to five dollars.

"I only have five left!" I snarled.

"Well… let me get that!" he said, looking crazy by the eyes. I forked over my last five dollars, and somehow, I knew I would never see that money again. When I earned that money, I had felt so accomplished. I was able to use what God had given me to my advantage, and now I felt so violated to have it snatched away. I knew what he'd spent the money on and it upset me even more than he thought he'd pulled the wool over my young eyes. But that wasn't the first time my father had used me for his own sick and twisted pleasure, and it indeed wouldn't be the last. I ran up to my room and cried myself to sleep.

The abuse I suffered from both of my parents delayed the time it took to grow up and eventually distance myself. Physically, I had finally distanced myself from my abusive, neglectful parents but I had no clue how broken and damaged I was walking away from those relationships. It started with those damn nightmares that became more frequent and severe. They were so vivid at times that I would awake from my sleep crying, my pajamas soaked with sweat and I would be frightened half to death. I don't have any clear memories of being raped only molested, but I keep having this reoccurring dream where I was being groped and inappropriately touched by different men. I'm between nine and twelve years old, and these are adult men, some old enough to be my father.

Chapter 3

BEEP! BEEP! BEEP! My alarm clock whaled and jolted me from yet another wretched nightmare. My t-shirt was damp with sweat. I then celebrated that familiar feeling of relief that it was just a bad dream. I peered to my right at the blaring alarm clock. It read nine-thirty a.m. "Shit!" I cursed to myself. I had a ten-a.m. appointment. I was a hairstylist and loved it. My first appointment was with Jackie, one of my most beloved and faithful clients. Jackie had begun coming to me a few years earlier, to get her hair done, when I landed my first job at a salon in Highland Park. She came every Saturday and girlfriend was serious about her hair. I scrambled to my feet and accidentally kicked over the glass of wine that I had been drinking the night before. "FUCK!" I yelled. I hated when I spilled things. I was so late, that clean-up would have to wait. I rushed to the shower. It seemed like I would scrub a layer of skin off trying to escape the dirty feeling I got every time I had one of those nightmares. I damn near busted my ass running from the shower to my room. I threw on a jogging suit, grabbed my purse and ran out of the door. When I finally arrived at the shop, I rushed in and immediately saw by my girl Jackie.

I thought I was going to have to come and look for you", she said shaking her head.

"Girl, I'm sorry it took me so long!"

"It must have been one of those nights." She snickered. Jackie had been a faithful client for quite some time, and we had a relationship. I styled her hair and scheduled her for the following week. The rest of the day went smoothly. I finished up and headed home.

I hadn't gotten up the stairs to my apartment when I heard my phone ringing. I scrambled for the keys to my apartment. I finally got the door open, and the phone stopped ringing. Shortly afterward my pager goes off. I reached the bottom of my junky purse to scavenge for it. I'd finally located it, and it read the number of my friend Omari Roman, whose nickname was "O," followed by the code 9-1-1. I hated it when he did that because it usually wasn't an emergency. He often really didn't want shit. I picked up the house phone and began to dial his number.

"Hello?" he said, as he picked up on the first ring.

"What's up?" I inquired.

"I just wanted to see if you wanted to get something to eat." He said.

"Okay, that's cool," I said, not feeling like leaving the house. O was so sweet, and I felt guilty for not being to him what he wanted me to be. I felt even worse for not being true to myself.

O was a guy I had met at a local bar while doing my favorite pass time…Karaoke. That night I was at the club with my girl Q. Q and I had been friends since kindergarten, and we were still quite close.. I was serious about singing and would do it as often and where ever I could. Whenever I sang, men and women alike were taken aback by my voice. I'd been singing since I was very young, and I utilized my gift to move people through song. The contribution of singing was the only meaningful thing my sperm donor ever gave me. That night I sang, Tamia's, "You Put a Move on My Heart". After singing I took a seat at the bar with my girl Q.

"Bitch sang that shit!" she shouted as we slapped five. I laughed.

Before we sat down good, the bartender came over and said, "Ol' boy said he got yawl, whatever yawl drinking." My drink of choice was Hennessey and coke, and Q ordered a vodka and cranberry. We continued to drink and talk shit all night. About the time we decided to head out, a man approached me. He was about six feet tall; dark-skinned; and muscular. "I sent you the drinks hoping you would accept my number later." He said. I smiled and thanked him for the drinks and reluctantly accepted his number. It was O.

O got to my house in what seemed like record time. I put my shoes back on and headed out of the door. I headed down the stairs with the heaviest conscience. I opened the passenger door, and a smiling face greeted me.

"Let's take a picture." He said with a grin.

"Huh?" I said, confused and half dazed.

"Picture us rolling!" he exclaimed, with his corny sense of humor. I couldn't help but laugh. For a man of his stature and serious looks, he had the most exciting sense of humor and gentle personality. During that time Starters Lounge was a place I frequented at the time. My favorite meal was the Delmonico steak and shrimp scampi, along with a Hennessy and coke. Starters had some of the best food in the city of Detroit as far as I was concerned. Within minutes I was feeling my drink, and the conversation was flowing. This was one of the few times it had been just the two of us, and he had a lot of questions, as did I. They were the usual questions.

"What school did you attend?"- "What do you do for a living?" - "Are you seeing anyone?"

"Well, there is one thing I should probably mention..." I began. His face went blank.

"What?" he hesitated to ask?

"I dance part-time," I revealed.

"You mean?" he began.

"Yes! That's precisely what I mean." I laughed, nervously. He played it cool.

"That's cool. I know lots of strippers." He said, trying to make me feel at ease. "In fact, I own a bar, and we have dancers on Sunday nights. You should come down and check it out." He suggested. I was reluctant, seeing as though I wasn't sure I wanted to go further with this guy. I always tried to make it a point not to lead anyone on. We called it a night, and he took me home.

Chapter 4

The following morning, I rolled off of the bed and onto the hard floor. Startled, I rolled onto my side, gasping for air. Again, I'd been awakened by a nightmare and was in a cold sweat. In the dream, I was just trying to get away, which explains my ending up on the floor. I got to my feet and looked down at the alarm clock on the other side of the bed. It read five twenty-two a.m. I could feel the vibration under my feet and hear the baseline of the music coming from the apartment below. *"What an asshole!"* I yelled in frustration. My neighbor directly below me was the most disgusting, lowlife, pig I'd ever met. As far as I was concerned, he was rude and ignorant! This motherfucker, with his raggedy ass, is up at five o'clock a.m., blasting this damn rap music, with his lazy ass. *"Some of us have to work, motherfucker."* I thought to myself as I angrily hopped back into bed, put the pillow over my head and tried, to no avail, to get back to sleep. Groggy from my shitty, half-assed night of sleep, I resented having to get up. I sluggishly dragged myself into the shower and turned it on. I was stunned as the ice-cold water hit me. *"What the fuck!"* I yelled as I stomped the surface of the tub. *"I got to get the fuck out of here,"* I said aloud. This raggedy ass apartment! The damn water finally warmed up just as I was about to step out, having washed my ass in the cold water. The day was already off to a bad start. I got dressed and headed to work.

I could get a cab on Greenfield in a heartbeat, but not today. They were passing me by like I was the plague. I began walking to work. I was so pissed that by the time I realized it I had made it work. I had angry-walked damn near the whole way to work, and it made no sense to get a cab. I walked into the shop and was greeted with a fake hello by the owner and her daughter. They weren't fond of me, and the feeling was mutual. She was one of those *"I'm old but think I'm young"* types, which was hilarious to me. The tension in the air was so thick, you could cut it with a knife, and I hated trying to work in an environment like that. It was time to move on. My search for a new salon began that day. I started trolling the yellow pages, want ads, and hair books.

Later that night, I packed my dance bag and headed to the club. I usually didn't go alone, but this night was different. I got there around nine o'clock that night and immediately went to the dressing room. There, I met with Tayvia and Kera. The two were cousins and had introduced me to the dance game. They were cool and sometimes we'd all go on out-of-town dance gigs together. Tayvia and I had become close, and we hung out quite often. At one point we were considered best friends. I didn't believe myself to be your average looking stripper. I stood five feet even; thick full hips; caramel complexion; one hundred thirty-five pounds; and slanted eyes that pierced through you that reminded you of the geisha girls. I finished my makeup and put on my favorite black pumps, along with a black G-string slingshot costume and matching garters. I slammed my locker shut and headed toward the stage. I heard the D.J. over the microphone say, "Beauty up Top!" That was my cue. I hit the stage and did my thing. The night was uneventful until a nigga I couldn't stand walked in. The fake-assed, want-to-be owner, "D." I hated this nigga with a passion. He was a rude, sexist prick. I hoped every night that someone would walk in that club and put holes in his tired ass. He hated me just as much. I did not attempt to hide what I thought of him.

"You better have my tip out at the end of the night, Beauty." He demanded.

"There must be another girl named Beauty here because you can't be talking' to me!" I snarled.

"Bitch, I am talking to you." He snapped, as he grabbed my arm and threw me to the floor. Startled, I rushed to my feet and charged at him. Before I could reach him, I was picked up off my feet by one colossal bouncer and carried to the dressing room.

"Get dressed Beauty and go home NOW!" he demanded. I dressed and grabbed my bag as I furiously rushed through the dressing room door. I was fusing and crying hysterically as the other dancers looked on. I never felt so helpless. I got home and cried myself to sleep.

Chapter 5

With my birthday quickly approaching I knew it was time for a fresh start. I would be turning twenty-one, and I knew I needed to make some significant changes in my life. I wanted a new place to live and work. I was finally ready to move on. While I tried to do new things, I couldn't help but reflect on the year-earlier that ultimately led to me being here. A few months earlier Tayvia suggested we go to Atlanta to celebrate. I was excited because it would be my first adult vacation with just me and my girlfriend. We invited other friends, but it turned out that only Tayvia and I were able to go. I didn't care I was ecstatic. It was one of the first times I felt in charge as an adult.

We landed in Atlanta, and I couldn't wait to hit the streets. Tayvia and I took our bags and settled into our hotel room at the Days Inn. We got a list of local clubs from the hotel concierge and hopped a cab to the nearest one. The line was a mile long, but that didn't deter us. Once inside, we began drinking like a fish. I was knocking the Hennessy back like a pro and Tayvia had one Long Island Iced Tea after another. While we danced to the music and sipped our drinks, we were approached by two men that introduced themselves as cousins. One guy began speaking in a thick Jamaican accent, "Hey baby, who are you here with." I pretended not to hear him. He came closer and repeated the same words once more.

"My friend" I replied dryly. His presence made me uncomfortable.

"How about we get something to eat?" he inquired, in a voice that was sort of hard for me to understand.

"What?" I yelled, over the loud reggae music. He repeated himself once more. "I don't know about that," I said, not wanting to go.

"Oh c'mon, Mone, (she always called me that) it'll be fun!" she tried to convince me, clutching the other man's arm. Still skeptical of the total strangers, I reluctantly agreed, not wanting to be a buzz-kill. "What's the worst that can happen?" I thought, feeling confident that I had my girl with me and wouldn't be alone.

After some convincing, we ended up at the Waffle House to get a bite to eat. The Waffle House is the South's version of Coney Island. I ordered, what had to be, the best buttery waffle, scrambled eggs, and a T-bone steak. We ate and chatted with the gentlemen we'd met earlier that night, and our trip seemed to be going well, thus far. After we were all full, one guy suggested that we go back to their apartment for drinks. Though the night was still pretty young, this notion was sobering to me. I wasn't feeling this shit at all. It's true what they say about peer pressure, though I was no follower. Tayvia practically begged me to agree, saying

"It's still early" "It's our first night here" "Please!" "I'm not ready to call it a night just yet." "Everything will be fine, I promise." Against my own better judgment, I agreed.

Once we were at the men's apartment, one of them, now identified as cousins, began to play music on an extensive stereo system. The other brought out a bottle of champagne and four glasses and handed each of us one. As we drank, I began to feel a little more relaxed. The one that was interested in me inched closer to me by the second until he sat close at my side. Tayvia sat across the room on a huge sectional sofa, nestled tightly to the other man. The guy that sat next to me was visibly drunk and was getting way too "free" with his hands for my taste. At first, I asked him politely to keep his hands to himself. He agreed and quickly apologized. Three seconds later, his hands were on my thigh again. This time, hoping he'd get it, I physically removed his hand and again asked him to stop. He continued to make sexual advances toward me, and I began to get scared. I begged him to keep his hands to himself, but my pleas fell on deaf ears. He was quite strong, and I was sure that he could easily overpower me if he wanted to. I tried to focus on the TV when I felt a wet, slimy feeling on my ear.

"What the fuck!" I exclaimed as he pulled back with a turned on look his face.

"Calm down now gal. I was just trying to get to know you." He tried to reassure me, in that thick accent, I could barely understand.

"Tayvia, let's go now!" I demanded. I heard no response. I'd been so busy trying to keep this guy at bay; I didn't notice that Tayvia had left the room, along with the other man. I began walking through the apartment, frantically searching for my friend. Much to my dismay, she had disappeared. Cell phones were having yet to become famous, and I was horrified that I had no way to contact her. A million thoughts raced through my mind. Had the other man kidnapped her? Harmed her? My thoughts began to terrify me. However, much to my relief, I returned to the living room to find my drunken, would-be rapist sound asleep. I guess the drinks he'd consumed that night had finally caught up with him. I exhaled. I search the house in a hurry to find the Yellow Pages. Once I did, I quickly scoured the taxicab section of the massive thick book. I saw one and dialed the number from the phone that was fastened to the kitchen wall.

Within minutes, I could hear the loud honking of the taxicab's horn in front of the apartment. I got into the taxi and sternly instructed the driver to take me to the Days Inn on Peachtree Street. He began driving for what seemed like forever. I finally arrived in front of the hotel and as I stepped out of the car. By the time I'd reached the hotel, it was well past six a.m. At that moment, I'd never been so thankful that the Lord had kept me safe. I attempted to go to the hotel room but got a reality check. I didn't have the key, and the room was in Tayvia's name. The desk clerk advised me that she would not be allowed to give me access to the hotel room, where MY things were. My name was nowhere on the reservation. It was then that I began to cry hysterically. I calmed down long enough to ask the clerk if I could use the phone. I dialed my mother, and I managed to get the words out as to my situation and what happened hours earlier. As furious now as I was, my mother demanded that I get to the airport and fly home immediately. She informed me that she would be wiring me some cash to do so. With the intention of doing just that, I took a seat in the lobby of the hotel to get my head together. Seeing the level of distress on my face, the clerk offered to, at best, open the door to the room for me to retrieve my things. On another note, now my fear for my friend had turned into anger. I couldn't believe that she would betray me and put, not only herself but also me in danger. We're six hundred miles from home, and she left me with a stranger and ran off with a stranger?! I was furious.

By now it was ten a.m., and after clearing my belongings from the hotel room, I headed back down to the lobby to call a cab. Just as I stepped off the elevator, Tayvia had the audacity to come strolling in. I was so livid that I couldn't speak. If I'd been a cartoon character, steam would've been coming from my ears and the top of my head. If looks could kill, she'd have dropped onto the floor. Again, tears began to roll down my already tear-stained face. Just then, this bitch had the balls to ask me "what's wrong, Mone?"

"Your behavior is what's wrong with me! Fuck you! I'm out!" I snapped. She grabbed my hand and began trying to pull me toward the elevator.

"Let my fucking arm go!" I shouted as the other hotel guest began to turn their heads and take notice. I was on fire, so, at that point, I didn't care who saw or heard.

"Please, Mone, don't leave." She pleaded. "I'm sorry! We were just going to talk." She tried to convince me. I heard none of it. I grabbed my things and headed for the door again as she pulled me in the opposite direction. She managed to get me near the elevator when she practically shoved me in. I resisted and scolded her during the elevator ride.

She coaxed and prodded me to return to the room with her. Feeling hurt, betrayed, and vulnerable all at once, I hesitantly gave in. I listened as she tried to explain away her actions. She must have noticed the skepticism on my face; something happened that I could never prepare for, Tayvia kissed me and continued to kiss me. The kisses were more erotic and more passionate than anyone had ever kissed me before. Much to my surprise, before I could give it much thought, I was kissing her back with an equal amount of passion and tenacity. She then began to fondle and caress my breasts, and her lips moved to my neck. Before long, she had her lips and tongue wrapped around my nipple. I could feel my juices begin to flow freely, and seconds later, my panties were wet. Her finger entered me, and I gasped and moaned with ecstasy. Before long, I could feel her lips around my clitoris. She was kissing my pussy just like she'd kissed my mouth moments earlier. I was damn near climbing the walls at this point. I wanted to make her feel as good, if not better than she was making me. I grabbed her shoulders and pulled her toward me to bring us face to face. We began to kiss again, and I could taste my juices on her lips. In one swift motion, I grabbed her hips and ass and sat her on my face. I began to move my tongue furiously, but softly on her clit. I went in every direction with my tongue, paying close attention to the sounds she made. I began to suck gently, and she moaned even louder.

"Oh, yes...Oh...Oh...Yes! Your tongue is deadly baby" she sang. "Don't Stop! Don't you dare stop!" she demanded of me as she exploded all over my face. Creamy goodness covered my chin and ran down the sides of my face as I laid on my back in sexual bliss. Up until then, that was the single most erotic moment of my life, and to my surprise, this felt so right. On top of that, I finally knew what it felt like to have an organism. I had secretly fantasized about sex with a woman. I didn't have much of a type, just that she had to have mad sex appeal and there had to be a powerful attraction. To be honest, I hadn't given much thought to any attraction to Tayvia, but she was sexy. She had milk chocolate skin that was smooth as silk. She had a shapely figure, with a small waist and ass for days. She had firm breasts and a smile with the cutest little gap. Tayvia and I had been friends, but she'd never given me any indication that she had any attraction to me, or any woman, for that matter. I'd have to say that this experience left me wanting more.

Chapter 6

Tayvia and I returned home to Detroit. A chill ran up my spine every time I thought of our encounter in Atlanta. I was overwhelmed with mixed emotions. Before my sexual encounter with Tayvia, I had never been with a woman, and I couldn't help but feel confused. She and I had been friends up to this point, and now I wasn't sure how to think of her. So many questions circled in my mind. Were we still just friends? Was she now my woman or just someone I would fuck? I was pretty confused at this point. However, I couldn't ignore my growing feelings for Tayvia. I went back and forth in my mind, trying to convince myself that it was ludicrous to think I could be in an actual relationship with another woman. I reasoned with myself that I "supposed" to be with and love a man. Just as I sat on my bed, contemplating the direction in which mine and Tayvia's friendship would go, I heard a horn honk in front of the apartment building. I stepped onto the balcony to see Tayvia's car parked out front. Just then, she exited the car and started up the walkway toward the building. I could hear her high heels clicking up the stairs as she made her way to the second floor. I took a moment to take it all in. There she stood, wearing black heels that tied up around her legs. She wore blue jean cut-off hot pants and a black shirt that revealed her perky cleavage. She was, also, rocking the quick-weave ponytail that I'd done for her just days earlier. Tayvia had stopped by to convince me to hang out with her. Considering how sexy she was looking it didn't take much convincing. I grabbed my purse and locked the front door behind me. We headed to her car and within minutes, pulled into the parking lot of one of our favorite spots to hang, Banko's Lounge, where I first began singing karaoke. Once inside, we went to the bar and ordered drinks. Once we had our cocktails, we chose a table closest to the stage. We sat and sipped, as we watched mostly tone-deaf singers hit the stage one after another. Just about the time, my ears started to bleed; a man approached our table. His eyes moved from me to Tayvia. "Hey baby, what's your name?" he asked. I had this guy pegged as a loser the minute he walked up. His hair was in cornrows to the back; his clothes were three sizes too big, and he had a beer bottle in one hand and a cigarette in the other. Tayvia, also, smoked like a locomotive, so I guess this didn't bother her.

"Tayvia," she said smiling ear to ear. "But you can call me Ms. Red." She advised.

"Okay, Ms. Red you look damn good. Can I buy you a drink?" he inquired.

"I'm drinking Vodka-N-Cranberry," she told him. Within minutes, he returned, glass in hand. I didn't know why at the time, but I was furious! Didn't he see me sitting there? How fucking rude of him to offer her a drink. I had to remind myself to play it cool. I wasn't even sure why this bothered me so much. I sat pep-talking myself in my head. *"Girl, I know you ain't tripping about a bitch!"* I said to myself, more confused than ever. *"Bitch, get it together."* I encouraged myself.

"I'll be back!" I suddenly announced, my attitude is very apparent in my voice. I snatched my purse from the table and headed for the bar. "Can I get a Hennessey and Coke? Please!" I demanded of the waitress. I could tell that there was a certain amount of rudeness in my request by the look the bartender returned to me. Nevertheless, she turned her back to me and began to pour the drink. She turned back towards me and said "six-fifty!" with the same amount of rudeness in her voice. I pulled a ten from my purse and handed it to her. She turned to the register briefly and then back towards me. She attempted to pass the change to me when I motioned for her to keep it as an unspoken apology for taking out my frustration on her. "Thank you!" she replied with a smile. I remember wishing I was leaving with her instead of the dick-crazy slut at the table.

I returned to the table to find it empty. My eyes scanned the room, but I found no Tayvia. I figured she'd gone to the ladies' room, so I sat down and began to sip my drink. While waiting on Tayvia, an untalented woman had taken center stage, and the song she was singing was almost unrecognizable. The sounds she made were horrible, almost similar to a cat being strangled. I was doing everything possible to avoid exploding in laughter, though I still struggled to remain calm and not think about my previous situation. Several minutes passed, and now that familiar feeling of worry was setting in. I got up and headed in the direction of the restroom. I went in, and there was the usual crowd of ratty women, gossiping and primping in the mirror. I went through, knocking on each stall door, but there was no Tayvia. I exited the restroom, and my eyes scanned the room once again. Now my worry had transformed to complete and utter panic. Once again, I began pep-talking myself to stay calm. I rushed toward the bar and placed an order with the same bartender from earlier that night.

"Can I have two shots of Hennessy with lemon wedges?" I requested. I made sure to be much politer this time, as I didn't want to come off rude as I had before. As she turned around to make my order, I began to scan her body with my eyes. She had a light-caramel complexion and the sexiest butterfly tattoo on the small of her well-toned back. She had wide hips, just like I liked, followed by thick, smooth thighs. The midriff-bearing top she wore showed off her tiny waist and displayed her shapely arms. She turned to me and quoted the price for the drinks, but I heard nothing. I was in a daze. She smiled, and the cutest dimple appeared on her left cheek. Her hair was shoulder length, and as she brushed it from her face, she repeated, "thirteen dollars, sweetie." I snapped out of my would-be fantasy and paid her for my drinks. "Thank you," I replied, feeling slightly embarrassed for undressing her with my eyes. I downed both shots and then ordered two more. Upon finishing my fourth shot, I was furious. I looked toward the entrance to the bar and in walks Tayvia, accompanied by "cornrows" himself. Her smile was broad as she walked with his arm around her waist. As I wondered where they were coming from, I rolled my eyes so hard, and it gave me a headache.

"Hey, Mone," she sang as she approached me.

"You had me worried," I began, with an obvious attitude in my voice. "You could've just told me you were going outside for a quickie," I growled.

"Damn, I'm sorry." she began.

"Are you ready?!" I interrupted. "I'm ready NOW!" I declared. I stormed toward the door. I looked back to see her saying her goodbyes to the dude then she followed. We got to the car, and I hopped inside. I still wasn't sure why her actions had such a profound effect on me. I was silent the entire ride home.

When we arrived at my apartment, I hurried up the stairs and opened the apartment door. Once inside, I began to undress as I headed for the shower. I turned it on and climbed in. Without hesitation, the confusion settled in and then the tears fell. I knew in my mind that I shouldn't be feeling this way, but I couldn't stop the tears from falling. Though I'd never expressed to Tayvia that I was developing feelings for her, I was heartbroken to learn that these emotions were not being reciprocated. I was never much for casual sex. Anytime I slept with someone before then; there were feelings and a relationship attached. Tayvia, on the other hand, just seemed to have no feelings at all. She had no problem going from man to man and treated our encounter like it never happened. I wasn't sure I was ready to go public with what we'd done either, but my mind, for some reason, stayed on only her. I finished my shower and climbed into bed.

The next morning, I awoke refreshed. I felt better and convinced myself that whatever feelings I harbored should remain repressed. I headed to work and did my daily routine. About the time for me to get off, Tayvia walked into the shop. I was a bit surprised, seeing as though the last time we saw each together didn't end so well.

"Hey Mone," she began. I didn't even look up, a sign that I was still bitter about the night before.

"Hey!" I answered, in the most solemn tone possible.

"Let's go to my house and watch movies." She suggested. Though I didn't want to show it, this made my day. I hesitated before saying "Okay," in the driest voice, trying not to evoke any emotion. I tidied up my, and we headed to her car. We pulled up to her house minutes later and went inside. Tayvia's house was always neat and clean. No one would ever suspect that she had three children. The kids were away, and her two roommates weren't home. We were there alone. We popped some corn and turned on the television. We'd gotten half-way through the first movie when someone knocked on the door. Tayvia rose from the couch and walked to the door. She peeped out of the peephole and quickly turned the lock to open the door. In walked a tall man. He was very light-skinned and looked, to me, to be bi-racial. He was handsome, resembled the singer, Jon B. He came in and took a seat on the further end of the couch. He spoke, just barely, to me and he seemed kind of shy. I said hello back and continued to watch the movie. We sat in silence as Tayvia disappeared into the bathroom. She had on short shorts and a t-shirt, but I could see mini water beads on her arms and legs, indicating that she'd been in the shower. She turned to head toward her bedroom and motioned for the gentleman to follow her. He complied, and they both went inside, closing the door behind them. I sat, confused, on the couch and tried to comprehend what was happening. I sat in disbelief for what seemed like an eternity. Suddenly, my blood began to boil. I was inconsolable. I reached for the phone on the table to my right and called Checker Cab. I gave the dispatcher the address and summoned a car. I began to gather my things, slinging and slamming things in anger. I rushed toward the bedroom door and gave it aloud, police-like knock. A naked Tayvia appeared through a cracked doorway and gave me a look as if to say, *"What the fuck do you want?"* My eyes shifted toward the bed, and I could see a shirtless man with the covers over him from the waist down. My eyes moved back to her in disgust.

"I'm out!" I declared, angrily, as I rushed toward the front door.

"Hold up, Mone," she began. "Why are you leaving'?" she asked. I gave her no response as I swung open the door and briskly shut it behind me. I boarded the cab and instructed the driver to my address.

I was furious at myself for being such a fool. I hated feeling like I was at a disadvantage. I allowed Tayvia to take me places, sexually and emotionally that I'd never let myself go before. I felt stupid because it appeared as if she was fucking every nigga she could get her hands on. How could I have been so stupid? Why didn't I see her for who she was, before now? I was pretty sure at this point that I wanted nothing more to do with this woman, romantically at least.

Chapter 7

I made a conscious decision to put the encounter between Tayvia and me behind me, but I realized that I still wanted to remain friends. She was a very caring and loyal person, at least within the capacity of platonic friendship. I saw no reason to hold our sexual indiscretions against her. After all, it's not like she put a gun to my head and forced me. We continued to hang out, and I was relieved to find that my feelings for her were starting to subside, and I felt confident that we could be friends. One particular night while we were out at a nightclub, I ran across a man that I'd met months earlier, named Que. He was a short, stocky guy and had a dark complexion. He occasionally sang; played keyboard; and D.J. at the local nightclubs. He initially had taken an interest in me after he saw me perform at Banko's Lounge. He was he was not my type physically but had a certain charm about him. We began dating and had become quite fond of each other. He was quite knowledgeable about the entertainment industry, and that made him interesting to me. Q's most redeeming quality was his ability to make me laugh, a definite must if you're seeking a potential date with me. He greeted Tayvia and I and offered us a round of drinks. We accepted and placed our order. We took our seats at the bar and began talking and drinking. Q slipped into a bar stool on the opposite side of me. He leaned in and began to caress my shoulders and back. He told me how beautiful I looked and how glad he was to see me. I had on tight black jeans and a form-fitting black sweater that showed off my ample cleavage. I wore knee-length black leather to match. My hair was in long black extensions, which I love, and the eyeliner was on just right to accentuate my eyes. He continued to stroke my ego, while Tayvia, on the other hand, was visibly pissed. I secretly wondered what her problem was, but I kept basking in the flow of compliments coming from the opposite direction. Q asked if we could meet for dinner the following day. After I agreed, he proceeded to walk away. Just then, I turned to notice Tayvia, apparently upset, with her arms folded in the seat next to me.

"Why do you like that nigga?" she snapped.

Stunned, I replied, "He's nice. What did he ever do to you?" She smacked her lips and rolled her eyes. Even more confused, "Why don't you like him?" I asked.

She retorted "because YOU like him!" As quickly as she said that, she got up, turned on her heels, and stormed out the bar. Now, I was dumbfounded. This was the same person who left me on her sofa feeling some way, while she fucked a nigga in the next room. Now she was reprimanding me for liking a guy who was wining and dining me. The nerve of her! I was confused, angry, and turned on all at the same time.

We abruptly ended the night, and I barely had time to close the car door before she sped off, leaving me in front of my apartment. I started up the stairs, not knowing how to feel about what had just taken palace.

I spent much of the night contemplating what I would say the next time I saw her. The following day was Sunday, so I didn't have to work. Most of the day, I lounged around the apartment alone in my pajamas trying to muster the courage to call Tayvia. I called her house but got no answer. I then paged her but got no response. I waited an hour or so and then paged again, and still, no answer. I began to worry, but thirty minutes later I paged her back, this time using a 9-1-1 code. A few moments later, the phone rang, and LaTayvia Lawson displayed across the screen. I quickly answered and asked in a panicked voice "Hello?" Are you okay?"

"Please don't ever call me that many times and use 9-1-1 unless you're dying!" She then hung up the telephone on me. All I heard was a dial tone. Wow! This bitch had balls of steel! She was rude to me for no reason, and she hung up on me? Now my feelings of confusion had quickly turned to anger and disgust. This woman was taking me on an emotional ride from hell, and I'd had enough. After that months would pass without Tayvia and me communicating.

Chapter 8

When 2001 arrived, I was finally ready to make moves. I set my sights on a new salon to work in as well as a better apartment to live in. Tasha was an old friend of my mom's, whom I referred to as Auntie Sasha. She and her twin sister, Sasha had owned a salon for quite some time. I'd heard rumors that Tasha had fallen off since Sasha abandoned the business and moved away. I'd spoken with Tasha about a month earlier and told her how unhappy I was with my current work environment. She had informed me that she could use some help and welcomed me with open arms. I gathered my things from the other salon and happily said my goodbyes. I moved into Auntie Tasha's salon the following week.

I settled in and began a friendship with one of the stylists named Alvin. He was a colorful character. Little did I know, he'd play an instrumental part in shaping me into the woman I am today. Alvin was gay; hilarious, and one of the most outrageous people I would ever meet. He loved to wear make-up, drink; and party. Alvin and I had an instant connection and soon began hanging together outside of work. He introduced me to the gay nightlife, and I was quickly a club regular. You could find us at some gay club around the metro area almost every weekend. There was *Regine's, The Rainbow Room, Stiletto's,* and *GiGi's,* just to name a few. Since Tayvia and I rarely hung out anymore, Alvin and I had become best buddies. He was sort of a male, gay version of her. They mirrored each other when it came to sexual appetite and the desire to sleep with as many men as possible. We would be out at the club, and I'd look up, and Alvin had gone off into the bathroom with a man he'd met only moments earlier. I found his antics comical at the time, but I'd soon learn that his behavior was no laughing matter.

I was happy at my new job and set out to find my new apartment. I successfully found a charming apartment near Dearborn. The neighborhood was peaceful, and the complex had a private pool. I was quite happy and doing so well for myself, especially after moving into such a beautiful place. I was only twenty-one, and I was doing quite well. There were people twice my age that wasn't living like I was. It was moving day, and O helped me move into my new apartment. The following week he took me shopping for new furniture. I selected a top of the line animal print sofa with a matching comfortable chair and a set of wrought-iron end tables with the coordinating coffee table. I picked out some high-end lamps and a few other accessories to complete the ensemble. I, also, purchased a wrought-iron king-sized canopy bed, complete with matching vanity and dresser. I'd already had my dining room suit from my other apartment, and it was still in fabulous shape. My apartment was laid, and most people were surprised that it was so well put together, being that I was so young.

I'd been in my apartment a few weeks, and things seemed to be taking shape. That weekend, Alvin and I planned to go out, and Stiletto's was the selected destination. Alvin brought along his young boy toy, an eighteen-year-old named Tomas. We arrived at the club and headed straight for the bar. I ordered the usual and Alvin ordered tequila. We drank one drink after another until we were what they call, *"full."* It was a good thing eighteen-year-old Tomas couldn't drink because we needed a designated driver.

Stiletto's was known for its fantastic drag shows, but we missed the show that night. Alvin and I just gotten our drinks and were headed to a table when I spotted the most beautiful woman in the club. She was probably the most beautiful woman I'd ever seen, but there was masculinity exuding from her. She was about five feet ten inches with a slim build. Her skin was caramel colored and smooth, and hazel eyes were mesmerizing, but I was captivated by her smile. She wore loose fitting jeans and a jersey style shirt with crisp white air force 1's. My panties were wet just at the sight of her. I could feel the butterflies wake up in my stomach as she looked up and caught me staring at her, yet I couldn't look away. I continued to give her the eye for what seemed like an eternity, and she started to walk in my direction. The slight nervousness

I was feeling had turned into sheer and utter panic. I tried to play it cool and not show it as I took a severe gulp from the drink I held in my hand.

"How are you doing'?" she asked.

"I'm good, and you?" I replied, trying to hide the anxiety in my voice.

"I saw you were giving me the eye, so I came over to talk to you." She stated.

Now the panic had turned to humiliation. I'm sure, at that moment, it showed all over my face. I laughed nervously and confessed, "Okay, you caught me."

"What's your name, sweetie?" She asked.

I answered "Shae."

"What's yours?" "Tiffanie," she replied. She had such a masculine aura about her, and it was shocking that she had such a dainty, feminine name. "That's a pretty name," I reassured her, hoping she would ask for my number.

"Well, Shae, can I call you sometime?" She asked. Yes! Just what I was waiting for, I thought to myself.

"Sure!" I eagerly replied as I rummaged through my purse for a pen. I located something to write with and wrote my name and pager number on the napkin in front of me. I folded it once and slipped it into her hand. She flashed that gorgeous smile and walked away.

Chapter 9

The summer was quickly passing by and things were finally going smoothly in my personal and professional life. I'd started a new job at a salon in Oak Park after the electricity had been shut off for non-payment at Sasha-N-Tasha's. Alvin followed close behind me because affiliating with Tasha had become quite detrimental to his health. As it turns out, Auntie Tasha was a stone-cold crack head and was leading Alvin back down the same road. I, also, discovered that Tiffanie was a broke thirty-one-year-old loser who was and still living with her mother, she had no job and was still fucking her ex. I dropped her with the quickness. The relationship with O and I had been on shaky ground after I met Tiffanie. Mainly because I ignored him. He'd been pretty much supporting me, paying most of my rent and bills. I insisted that I wanted no parts of a commitment with him, but I guess in his mind, things would turn around.

A new spot had opened downtown, called the *Parabox*. Though I no longer wanted to be serious with Tiffanie, Alvin and I agreed to come and watch her perform at the new club. We arrived, and Tiffanie was on stage. I concluded that she was a loser, but damn, she was so sexy. I began getting tempted to sleep with her again, and after careful consideration, I talked myself out of it. Just then, my eyes shifted across the crowded room to the bar. Alvin was on the dance floor doing his best kick and split, so I took the opportunity to go and enjoy a drink. I reached the bar and just as I got the bartender's attention, someone else got mine.

"Hey, Beautiful," I heard a soft-deep voice say. I turned my attention in the direction of the sound to see a petite, light-brown skinned woman next to me. I smiled at her. She wasn't much taller than me, about 5'3" and she had a pretty smile, curly black hair that was cropped short, and eyelashes that went on forever. She had a slightly masculine way about her kind of like a well-dressed teenaged boy, and she wore clothing that fit the part.

"Are you here by yourself?" She inquired.

"No, my best friend is out on the dance floor," I answered.

"I was just about to order. Would you like something to drink?" I asked her. She looked back at me in shock.

"Sure." She stated with the same amount of surprise in her voice. I ordered for us both, and we each took a seat side by side at the bar.

"So, what's your name? I asked, attempting to initiate conversation. "Angela, "she replied, "but most people call me Tiny."

"Well, "I began, "I like Angela. Can I call you that?" I declared.

"Call me whichever you prefer." She replied. Angela was articulate, charming, and from what I could tell so far, sweet. A far cry from the last piece of work I'd dated. We continued to sip and talk for much of the night. About the time for the club to close, she asked if she could have my number. I happily obliged and told her to call me the following day.

Angela called me the very next day, and we decided to meet in Mexican town for dinner. The conversation was an interesting and stimulating one. I learned that she was adopted as an infant and was now raising a sibling of hers. She worked for the City of Detroit and was currently trying to fit going back to college into her hectic schedule. If there was one thing I could identify with her on, it was the feelings of abandonment as a child. Yes. I knew that all too well.

For that entire summer, Angela and I continued to see each other. We'd begun to get to know each other quite well, and she introduced me to her eleven-year-old sister, who she'd been raising. Myesha was a pretty little girl. She had smooth dark skin and curly black hair kind of like I'd always imagined my daughter would look. I often had this ghost of a child in the back of my mind, just another lousy memory I couldn't seem to escape.

Angela had been the only one I was currently seeing. O was still in the background, but he was not happy with the idea of my new-found friend. He knew she was moving in on me and it was plain now that the chances of me being with him were slim to none. I was spending every spare moment with Angela. I'll admit that I was a little selfish, seeing as though he was paying a considerable amount of my bills...or so I thought.

I returned home one evening from a date with Angela to find an eviction notice on my apartment door. I fumbled for my keys and unlocked it. I stormed inside and slammed my purse onto the coffee table. I went straight to the phone. I angrily punched the keys as I dialed O's number. *"The nerve of that fat bastard,"* I thought to myself as I waited for him to pick up. Once he did, I wasted no time letting his ass have it. "What the FUCK?" I began. I gave him the third degree, and when finally given the opportunity to speak, he calmly reassured me that he would take care of everything. This gave me some measure of comfort, but I was still mad as hell. I'd rationalized in my mind that I'd never asked O for any of these things. He'd just done them because he wanted to, never mind his reasons. To me, that meant my actions were justified, coupled with the fact that I'd specified to him on several occasions that he and I were not a couple.

Chapter 10

I'd planned to go with Alvin to the Parabox that Saturday after work with our new friend, Janeen. We'd all brought our go-out clothes to work with us, and after the last customer left, we got ready for the night. We arrived at the club, and it was banging. The music was loud, and the line was wrapped around the building. Once inside, we all made a beeline for the bar. We each ordered a cocktail and began to get full. I was pleasantly surprised to spot Angela at the end of the bar. I proceeded toward her and wrapped my arms around her neck and planted one. I wanted to do her right there on the bar. I hadn't had sex since breaking up with Tiffanie. We smooched and patted each other all night until she finally asked, "You coming home with me tonight?"

"Hell yeah, I eagerly replied. I waved goodbye to my friends, and Angela and I headed to her car.

During the car ride to her place, I was full of anticipation. My mind and body tingled with anticipation that I was sure I'd wet her seat. We pulled up to her apartment, and my mind raced with erotic thoughts. She opened the door and led me in. The apartment was dark, and it seemed to be just the two of us there.

"Where's Myesha?" I asked.

"She's at my aunts' for the weekend." She replied. She turned on the lights and proceeded to the kitchen. She returned to the living room with a glass in each hand. We sat down and began to sip our night-cap as we engaged in light conversation.

She began to ease closer to me and soon her hand was on my dress. She began to kiss me furiously, and this excited me even more. She kissed my neck softly and then lowered herself to my breasts. She kissed them tenderly, one after the other, slightly squeezing them at the same time. She was soon at my belly button, and she licked it inside and out, and I could feel my belly ring shifting with each flick of her tongue. My heart raced as I felt her move down to my pubic line. Suddenly I felt her tongue plunge into my vaginal opening. She twirled around my clitoris, and it began to pulsate with sensation. I cried out in ecstasy. I sighed as I grabbed the top of her head, pushing her further inside. I could feel her lips gently sucking every part of my womanhood as I moaned aloud, reassuring her that she was doing the damn thang. Suddenly she stopped, just as I was about to climax.

"Hold up. I'll be right back," She whispered. I was confused and the slightest bit angry. "Did she just take a bathroom break in the middle of giving me good head?" I thought to myself. "I think she just did," I began to convince myself. Just as I was putting on my (this some bullshit) face, she returned to the living room. The room was now dark again, and the only light that shone was the tiny green indicator and digital clock on the VCR. I could vaguely see what appeared to be a belt around her naked waist, but I wasn't sure. In one swift motion, she was back on top of me, and she began to kiss me again. I could taste my juices on her tongue. Suddenly, I felt a firm, but flexible object enters me. Ughhh! I cried out, with both surprise and pleasure. She began to thrust in and out. Oh my god! She was fucking me and better than any nigga ever had. I'd always liked the feeling of penetration, but not necessarily the male presence attached to it. She began thrusting harder and harder. But now, she'd thrown my legs over her shoulders, and she was fucking me so well I was serenading the neighbors. She gave me one last powerful thrust, and I felt myself explode. She collapsed on top of me, and I could feel a light mist of perspiration on her body. She began to kiss me softly as I lay there in a state of shock. How could this {woman} possibly fuck me? How could she fuck me better than any of the men I'd ever been with sexually? I was in awe, and I knew I could never let her go. After that, things flowed smoothly between Angela and me. However, she had not officially asked me to be her girl, but I was confident that we saw each other exclusively.

Chapter 11

Janeen and I planned a trip to Toronto, Canada for the annual Caribbean festival. Janeen was from Trinidad; she spoke with a thick Caribbean accent that most people found so sexy and unique. I looked at her like a sister. She was married to the owner of the salon at which I worked. He was an old, white undercover racist asshole named Ben Powell. He pretended to like black people, but really, he looked down upon us. The word "nigger" was the first to roll off of his tongue whenever he and Janeen argued. I imagined she put up with him because she saw him as wealthy and powerful. I'd later find out just how true this was. I asked Kera to come along to with us. Janeen invited a friend named John, who already had a room on reserve and suggested that we could stay with him. I was automatically leery and distrustful of men, but for some reason, John didn't give me ill vibes. He was cool from the jump, and he never tried to hit on us or got all excited like he'd never seen women before like most guys I'd come in contact with usually behaved.

The four of us arrived in Toronto at 10 a.m. after a hot and miserable four-hour drive. We checked into the hotel and proceeded to our room.

We settled in and began to plan for the day. Janeen wanted to hit the festival immediately; the festivities reminded her of celebrations back home. We all decided to get a bite to eat and do some light shopping first. After we did that, we got directions from a cashier and headed to the festival. We turned onto the street where the fairgrounds were located and began to look for a space to park the car. The roads were covered with people of all shapes, sizes, ethnicities, and walks of life. This festival was colossal, far beyond anything I'd ever seen at home. As we happened upon what seemed to be the only available parking, I started to experience a strange feeling in both my stomach and my mind. I looked a few paces to my right and was shocked at what was before me. It was Angela, my girl, hugged up and holding hands with some chick. My mouth hit the floor. I was stunned. My friends knew Angela and had taken notice as well.

"I'll be damned!" Janeen said, cupping her mouth.

"This is unbelievable!" Kera exclaimed.

"That's the same girl who came to the shop and asked for you last week!" Janeen said, referring to the light-skinned, thick girl holding Angela's hand. "She claimed she wanted to make a hair appointment, but you were out that day!" Janeen informed me, shaking her head.

"Did she say her name?" I anxiously inquired.

"Yeah...Kitty," Janeen replied. How familiar this name was to me? This was the name of Angela's ex. I'd found out during one of our long conversations that she'd been romantically involved with Kitty the year earlier. She went on about their relationship and how she'd chosen to end it as a result of Kitty's cheating and borderline psycho ways. Here she was, cheating on me with her. We never said we were not official, but I thought that we were headed in that direction.

"Let me out!" I shouted angrily as a few bystanders turned to investigate the commotion coming from the car. Janeen quickly pressed the lock and held it, trapping me in the back seat. Kera began to tug at my arm, urging me to remain inside the car. "Let me the fuck GO!" I demanded as she pulled even harder in the opposite direction. Janeen quickly threw the car into drive and sped off. "Why didn't y'all let me at that bitch?" I growled as tears began to stream down my face.

"Calm down, Shae!" Janeen began.

"Yeah, girl, it's not worth it," Kera continued. I was inconsolable.

Was this what I had to look forward to in my future relationships? Why was it that all of the people who claimed to care for me hurt me or abandoned me or both? I sobbed as I hung my head in despair and disbelief. I moped around for the remaining days of the trip, unable to enjoy myself. I was just ready to go home and try to put the whole thing behind me. I'd decided that Angela and I were through and after I scolded her in the nastiest voicemail message, I wanted to delete her from my phone and my memory.

Chapter 12

I returned home and started up the stairs to my apartment. I inserted the key and attempted to turn it, but it would not. I wiggled it a little, thinking it may be stuck. I tried to turn it and was, once again, unsuccessful. Confused, I fumbled through the other keys on my ring and found a similar looking key. I tried that key, and it did not open the lock either. I headed down the back staircase toward the rental office. I reached the bottom of the stairwell, and much to my dismay, I saw what looked to be my sofa outside in the rear of the building. My eyes scanned the street, and all of my possessions were strewn about the lawn. How could this be happening? I cried as I speed-walked to the leasing center.

"What the hell is going on?" I demanded of the woman behind the desk.

"Ma'am, calm down before I'm forced to call the police on you." She warned. At that point, that didn't scare me, and there was no calming me down.

"No, fuck that! Why the FUCK is my shit all over the fucking lawn?" I retorted. She turned her back to me and pulled a manila envelope from a drawer. She slapped it down on the desk in front of me. She gave me a look as if to say "well...open it." I did and was horrified to find several notices to quit" forms, all of which I was not familiar with, along with multiple returned checks that bore the signature "Omari Roman," O's government name. I could feel my blood begin to boil. How could I have been so stupid? I was angry at myself for trusting a nigga; after all, what reason did I have to do so? I was furious! He'd assured me that everything was taken care of and all the while he knew an eviction was in process. He was angry at me for having chosen a woman over him, and he'd decided to make me pay for it. I began calling him repeatedly, all to no avail. He knew what was going on; he was listed on my lease as an emergency contact and was authorized to pay my bills. Still, he'd chosen to ignore my calls. I was livid and crying uncontrollably.

I walked out to try and salvage what was left of my things. Onlookers had already rummaged through it and had stolen electronics and other valuables. I was floored. I'd never been evicted or seen it done before and, in my mind, this was the worst thing that could ever happen. I called Janeen, and she arrived in her had a pick-up truck. She had come to help me retrieve what I could. We gathered as many things as the truck would hold and left the complex. I'd called my sperm donor and told him that I needed to come and crash there. He eagerly agreed. He thought he'd use me to pay the rent and bills while he smoked his SSI check. Technically, the house was mine, when my grandmother passed away she willed it to me. I knew all he saw was as an opportunity for a free ride. That evening, I moved my things into the upstairs bedroom at the house. I looked around and, much to my dismay, the house was almost unrecognizable. It seemed nothing like the pleasant and safe environment I remembered as a child. It was run down, and there were all kinds of unsavory people hanging around at all times of the night and day. He'd managed to destroy what was once a good, stable situation. I resented him because everything my father touched was turned to shit?

As I lay on the sofa, I couldn't help but feel devastated by all the events of the past few months. I quickly wiped the tears from my eyes, not wanting to be vulnerable or have feelings of self-pity. I laid there and began to doze off. Without giving it much thought, I slipped my hand into my pajama pants. I started to caress my genitals. In an instant, I found myself masturbating. I massaged my clitoris vigorously, and before long, I could feel that familiar sensation. My muscles began to contract as I felt a wet burst squirt onto my fingers. I lay there exhausted; feeling like the wind had been knocked right out of me. I always felt guilty after masturbating, and I didn't know why. I'd had the urge to do it often since about the age of five. I could never understand why I was so sexually charged at such a young age, being that I'd never had a sexual experience at that time. I'd had a fascination with sex for as far back as I could remember, and I had no explanation for this, being that I'd never witnessed, heard of, or performed a sexual act in my early life. After moving back in with my dad, the nightmares became more and even more vivid, and this frightened me. Most of the time, in the dream, I was physically touched by a man. In almost every instance, I was young, usually between the ages of nine and twelve. I knew that the men in the dreams were all adults, some even old enough to be my father. In the dreams, I was always being groped and kissed by them, and they would handle me roughly. I had no idea what was causing these explicit dreams.

I stayed to myself in my second-floor bedroom at home I now shared with my father. Each day after work, I cringed at the very idea of having to go back there. I was used to a quiet and peaceful dwelling, and this was anything but that. It was a glorified crack house, and I was terrified all the time. My sperm donor claimed that he was looking for an apartment and that he would be moving out soon. Again, just lies he used to manipulate me. He was always so good at doing just that.

For whatever reason, since I'd come to stay in this house, horrible memories started to come to light, as did the nightmares. I didn't like the sick feeling in my stomach that I got every time I pulled up to that house. I had to come up with a plan to get out of there…and fast. One of the memories I vividly recall is going to church on Sunday with him and my grandmother. My grandmother was a devout Christian, and she insisted that we develop a healthy relationship with GOD. One Sunday after we arrived at the church, my father pulled me aside and asked me a favor. "When Pastor Shaw starts the benediction, you and Tashena come out to the bathroom." He instructed. During that time, I felt a great deal of intimidation when it came to my father. Therefore, no questions were asked, I agreed. I had three friends at church named Tashena; Tabitha; and Tanya. We were all members of the youth choir committee along with my grandmother, and that's how we became great friends. I looked up to Tashena, much like an older sister. I had no older siblings, and she'd become the closest thing to that. She was about twelve at the time. I know this because I can recall her being approximately four years my senior, making me about eight.

I did as I instructed and when the benediction began, I whispered to Shena "C'mon, let's go to the bathroom." She agreed, and we started out of the sanctuary doors to the main hallway. We bent the corner and started up the corridor that led to the ladies' bathroom. Just off of the ladies' room was a small booth that held the church pay phone. We were startled when out from the booth, popped my father. He took Shena by the hand and led her into the booth. He began kissing her, using his tongue. He groped and caressed her developed body. I can remember standing there in the empty hallway, frozen, watching my thirty-year-old father make out with my twelve-year-old friend. He'd convinced me that he was of no wrongdoing and that because of the difference in our ages, that he could very well marry her and make her my stepmother.

Chapter 13

One day after work, Janeen suggested that we go to Palmer Park. Palmer Park was a local hang out spot that members of the gay community frequented. I was all for it since I wanted any ole excuse not to go home. We stopped at the liquor store on the way there and purchased a liter of Paul Mason brandy and a large bottle of Coca-Cola. We mixed our drinks in the car and headed to the park. Once there, we found a space in the most popular section and parked the car. We sipped and chatted as we laughed and made fun of some of the hilarious characters that could be seen on any given day at the park. There were all kinds of things going on. People were blasting their car stereos as people sand and danced along. There were transgender people, female and male alike. Then there were people who you'd never suspect of being gay just at the sight of them. There was a plethora of L.G.B.T. people all hanging out together and happy to be in an environment where they could finally be comfortable in their skin. Living an authentic life isn't an option for some people, and I didn't take that lightly

As we sat and sipped, Janeen called to my attention a car that sat a few spaces down from us. It was a royal blue 1980's Camaro with a roof, identical to the one Angela drove. My blood began to boil as I recalled the recent events concerning her. I started to mentally replay how she'd deceived me and all along was still seeing her ex while having me believe that I was the only one she was seeing. I was furious all over again. I began to gulp my drink and pretty soon I felt an eerie calm cover over me. Through my peripheral vision, I could see a petite figure approaching the car. "Oh shit!" Janeen said. "Don't look now but she's coming this way." In no time, I felt a tap on my shoulder through the open passenger window. I turned my head, and there stood Angela. She had a look on her face that spelled sadness, remorse, fear, and anxiety all at the same time.

"Can I please talk to you for a second?" She began. I rolled my eyes and folded my arms.

I sarcastically asked, "About what?"

"I made a huge mistake" She started again. She began to pour out her heart to me, telling me that she was so sorry for not being honest with me and that she just wanted to make sure that there was no unfinished business between her and Kitty. I felt my eyes well up. I attempted to play hard, but the truth was, I had significant feelings for this girl. I could see myself being her woman and us having a future together. I was young, but in my mind, I was ready to give myself to her. After a conversation that went on for what seemed like forever, Angela and I reconciled. We agreed to put the past behind us and start fresh with a clean slate. Upon this decision, she asked me to move in with her and Myesha. I happily agreed and wasted no time jumping out of that God-forsaken hellhole I resided in.

Chapter 14

And so, our life together began. For about the next year, things were going well between us. I assumed the role of stepmother to Myesha, and she and I formed quite a bond. I was hands-on with her, attending parent-teacher meetings regularly, as well as taking her to and from school, and meeting most of her parental needs. I was surprised at how maternal I was, being that I had no biological children of my own. I'd become pregnant in high school, by my first boyfriend, at the age of seventeen, but was forced by my mother to have an abortion, something that went against everything I believed in.

I'd found out earlier in our relationship that Angela and Myesha's mother, Jeanette, struggled with drug addiction, rendering her unable to care for young Myesha properly. I'd, also, learned that Angela had two older brothers, who had both been victims of random street violence. They were both shot and killed as teenagers. My heart ached, and I couldn't imagine what it must be like for a mother to lose not one, but two of her children. The plan was that Jeanette would undergo substance abuse treatment and parenting classes. Once she completed this, Myesha would return to her custody. For now, Angela and I would assume the role of her custodians.

I awoke early one morning to find Angela still in bed. She was usually already gone to work by the time I woke up and started my day. I went to wake Myesha and make sure she started to get ready for school. The morning went without incident as I maintained my usual routine. I dropped Myesha at school and headed to the salon. Upon arriving, I set up my workstation and prepared to serve the clients of the day. About eleven 0'Clock, the salon phone began to ring. "

Parisian Salon, how may I direct your call?" I asked into the receiver. On the other end was a voice I recognized, but a frantic tone accompanied it. I could barely understand her as she tried to explain the events taking place at the other end of the phone. "Slow down so I can understand what you're saying." I pleaded, trying to calm her down. It was Angela on the other end of the line, and she was hysterical.

"Alvin is here, and I'm trying to stop the bleeding!" She cried.

"Okay baby…slow down and tell me what happened," I coached.

"He showed up here and asked to use the bathroom. I said sure and invited him in. When he didn't come out after a half an hour, I knocked on the door to make sure he was ok. He didn't answer so I cracked the door. I found him lying on the bathroom floor, unconscious. I rolled him over there was a pool of blood. I started to scream. I grabbed his arms and noticed the blood coming from his wrists. I stumbled to the phone and called 9-1-1. I'm still trying to stop the bleeding. The ambulance is on the way." She explained. Oh my god! My best friend was at my house attempting to commit suicide. I had to get home and fast! I hung up from my distraught girlfriend and raced back.

By the time I pulled into the parking lot of our building, I was shaking. I exited the car and ran in. I ran up the stairs and rushed through the apartment door. I found the apartment empty after checking every room. I glanced into the main bathroom to see the evidence of the events that had taken place moments earlier. There was a small amount of blood in the sink and a puddle of blood on the floor. I immediately went to the phone and dialed Angela's cell. "Baby, where are you?" I anxiously questioned her.

"He's been admitted to Receiving Hospital." She answered. I wasted no time heading to the hospital to make sure my friend and my woman were okay.

Chapter 15

After having our apartment broken into several times, Angela and I decided to move to a more affluent part of the city. At this time, any property west of Telegraph Road was considered a hot commodity, so we found a place off Seven Mile Road, just west of Telegraph. It was a beautiful apartment, complete with a courtyard and swimming pool. It was peaceful, and the complex housed mostly older and more established people. I had, also, started a new job, because the last salon I worked at closed. The salon closed because Janeen had begun to explore her bisexual curiosities and after her husband got wind of this, he punished her by closing the salon, thus, ultimately snatching the carpet from under her feet. He wasn't happy with the friendship she'd developed with us either because he wasn't all that fond of black people. For some reason, he didn't see Janeen as black. He instilled in her that because she was from Trinidad, she too was superior to African-Americans and he wanted to keep her oblivious to the real world. It was only when she'd make him angry that she was conveniently on the same "low class" level as us, and he let her know it in no uncertain terms. I'm now set up shop at a salon on Fenkell Avenue.

I headed to work that Friday morning, Myesha in tow. We arrived about ten a.m. and went inside. Not much was out of the ordinary that day, so I set up as usual and prepared to get to work. The day was going smoothly, and about one in the afternoon, one of my favorite clients showed up at the salon her name was Treecy. She had three adolescent daughters and had recently become engaged to be married. Her eldest daughter, Danita sometimes filled in as my shampoo assistant on the hectic weekends. "Girl, I need you to hook me up a nice up-do. Mike and I are going to Toledo to get married tomorrow," she explained.

"Congratulations!" I exclaimed. "I'm so happy for you." She beamed and blushed with a smile from ear to ear. "Sit on down. I got u." I instructed. She did, and I got to work on what was sure to be a bridal masterpiece. I was always very good at creating elegant styles that complimented one's features as well as their purpose. I was in the groove when a tall gentleman appeared in the salon doorway. Everyone turned to see what he wanted.

"Anybody own a grey cutlass?" He inquired.

"That's my car!" I quickly replied, now anxious.

"Somebody just hit it," He informed, as he turned on his heels and left the salon. Without hesitation, I hurried out of the building to inspect the damage to my car. Upon walking up to it, nothing could prepare me for what would happen next. I heard Myesha's voice, in what seemed to be a panicked state. She'd now followed me outside. "Shae watch out!"

She yelled. Suddenly I could feel what felt like a hard poke in my left shoulder blade, followed by an intense burning sensation. I tried to turn around, but I then felt a forceful blow across my shoulders from what felt like a massive blunt object. I hadn't grasped what was happening, but my first instinct was to try to protect my head and upper body. I could tell by this point that I was outnumbered, and I rolled into a ball on the ground. I felt a second sharp plunge into my back, much like the first. I looked up to see at least three women with rags covering their faces, and just the portion where their eyes were, was cut out. I thought I was dreaming. How could this possibly be happening? One woman was violently jabbing at my upper frontal body. She'd already landed two stab wounds to my left forearm and was now aiming for my chest and abdomen. The thick apron that I wore to protect my clothes when I did hair was the only thing shielding me from her vigorous attempts. Still, she tried to no avail. The attack seemed to go on forever and, suddenly, it stopped. The women then fled the scene in a blue two-door car that bore no license plate.

By now, everyone in the shop had come outside to investigate the commotion. Treecy, a registered nurse, helped me to my feet and threw my arm across her shoulders. She guided me into the salon and instructed me to lie down on the floor. I felt a cold, wet sensation between my legs. The sheer and utter terror of the events minutes earlier had caused my bladder to release. I began to feel cold all over and the noise faded.

"She's going into shock!" I heard Treecy shout. Though I was told I never lost consciousness, the next few moments, still to this day, remain a blur. I remember being loaded into the ambulance and being asked a battery or questions by the E.M.T I answered them to the best of my knowledge on the seemingly most interminable ride ever to the hospital. I arrived at Sinai Grace Hospital, where my mother and police met me. My mother had tears in her eyes as the police and hospital staff attempted to evaluate me. Seeing my mother emotional surprised me because I'd never really seen my mother display much emotion, even as a child. My mother could be quite cold at times. She would get angry and violent and rarely ever showed much empathy or maternal compassion. It seemed to me, as a youth, that she only had affection for one person…her man.

Chapter 16

After I was attacked, I struggled to return to a "normal" sense of life. This was virtually impossible, being that all of the symptoms of my post-traumatic stress disorder were as evident as ever. Every loud noise, a stranger walking close to me, or even a simple knock at the door sent me into a frenzy of emotion. I was a nervous wreck and scared to leave my house. I stayed barricaded in my apartment and nursed my physical and emotional wounds. I came away with a total of four stab wounds, but the emotional scars ran much more in-depth. I couldn't return to my job, being that it was the scene of my horrific ordeal. I couldn't work for about four months, due to my injuries and also my extreme state of paranoia.

Angela and I began to argue more and more. I don't think she could even begin to understand the changes I was going through. In a heated argument, she told me to get over it and also accused me of being selfish, lazy, and unwilling to work. She said that I was using my injuries as an excuse to sponge off of her and even told me that I'd brought it on myself. This devastated me. How could she be so cruel and insensitive? This created a tremendous amount of resentment toward her and ultimately sent our relationship on a rapid downward spiral. I fell into a deep depression. My eyes began to swell from the endless crying. I was petrified of people and having horrifying nightmares. I had lost all desire to do the things that I loved most. My business plummeted, and I rarely ever left the house. Angela and I barely even spoke, and I was pretty sure now that she was cheating on me.

My condition continued to decline, and I began to experience hallucinations. I would swear people were following me and I had constant flashbacks of that day. The mere sight of any blue car made me lose it. I never saw the faces of and couldn't identify my attackers, and that made me feel worst. I had the frightening idea all the time that they could be right next to me, and I wouldn't even know it. I began to question my faith in God. "Lord, Why me?" I'd ask. "Don't you love me? What did I do to deserve this?" I constantly wondered.

One day, I awoke but had the most challenging time pulling myself out of bed. Angela had already left for work, and I usually would get up, have breakfast, and shower, at the very least. This particular morning was very different. For some reason, I felt no motivation to leave my room. My heart began to feel very heavy, and the tears started to flow instantaneously. My ears were soon pools of tears, and as I stared at the ceiling, I began to feel the will to live slipping from me. My eyes scanned the room and then landed beside me. On the nightstand to my left was a bottle of pills. One by one I began to swallow until the bottle was empty. As the tears continued, I began to drift off to sleep.

"Can you hear me?!" I heard a voice yell. I tried, but I couldn't speak. I wanted to answer, but the words wouldn't come out. "Shae wake up, baby please!" The voice shouted again. I looked at my feet and saw a frantic Angela scrambling to place my shoes on my feet. Next, she grabbed a jacket and threw it across my shoulders as she threw my arm around her neck. She instructed me to try to stand as she lifted me off the bed. With her as my crutch, I attempted to stagger to the front door, while slumped across her shoulders. "We got to get you to the hospital." I heard her say. We made our way down the stairs and to the parking lot. She laid me on the back seat of the car, and I began to drift off again. "Stay with me, baby!" She called to me from the driver's seat. "Stay awake, for me baby." She said. The panic was apparent in her voice. In what seemed like seconds, the floodlights that lined the awning of the emergency entrance of Sinai Grace Hospital shone through the car window. "I need a wheelchair!" I heard Angela's voice shout. She'd come around to the back-passenger door and flung it open. She grabbed my arms and began to pull me from the car. I struggled to my feet and tried to ease into the wheelchair. Angela wheeled me into the emergency room and ran to the front desk. She held up the empty bottle that once contained the pills that I ingested earlier that day. I had no idea how much time had elapsed since I took what I was sure to be the fatal dose, but by this time, the night sky was pitch black. Angela explained to the nurse that I'd taken the pills, which I now knew were over the counter Ibuprofen. I had no idea why I wasn't dead.

I was immediately rushed through the triage doors and put into an examination room. This was shocking because of all the times I'd been to this death trap. I never got seen this fast, including when I was stabbed. After a few minutes, a short, stout, Asian Indian man stuck his head into the curtain. He took one look at what I assumed was my chart and called to another hospital employee. Another man, black man, entered the curtain. He was tall and dark-skinned and beneath his scrub uniform was a physique that resembled that of a bodybuilder. He looked as if he could lift me, Angela, and the short Indian doctor all at once if he so decided. He held in his hand, what looked to be, restraints. He walked to my bedside and grabbed my left wrist firmly in his hands. He began to attach the strap to my wrist and then to the bed rail.

"Wait a minute," I began, frantically, my speech still a bit slurred. I looked at Angela who'd had risen from her seat.

"Hey, man, what are doing'?" She demanded.

He looked at her and said, "Standard procedure, ma'am so she doesn't hurt herself again." He continued. "Her paperwork says suicide watch." OMG! I'm going' to the fucking looney bin, I thought. I panicked and began to cry. He strapped my other arm, and with his size and strength, I knew better than to put up a fight. "Calm down." He whispered. "I'll come back and take them off in a little while if you stay calm." He assured me.

I laid there helpless for what seemed like hours. Angela left the room to make phone calls. Among those notified was my mother. I wasn't sure what Angela told her, but she never bothered to come. That hurt me, but I'd never let her know that. After a few minutes, Angela returned. She opened a cranberry juice that she held in her hand and put it to my lips. I felt like I hadn't eaten or drank anything for years as the cold, sweet liquid hit my lips. My eyelids were heavy, and I began to drift once more. Just as I nodded off the gentleman that had strapped me to the bed as a mental patient returned to the room. He removed the restraints, as promised, and took a thin, transparent elongated tube from a drawer beside me. "Take a deep breath." He instructed me, and as I did so, he shoved the tube down my throat. I gagged and tasted vomit on my tongue. "We got to pump your stomach, little lady." He warned too late. I was dizzy all of a sudden and began to vomit uncontrollably for the next few minutes. I was in excruciating pain from head to toe, and my body shook with chills and agony. By this time, there were other nurses and the short Indian doctor surrounding me. I felt like I'd been hit by a truck.

Just when I thought my ordeal was over, a tall, slim black woman entered the room. She was light-skinned and wore thin, wire-framed glasses. Her hair was pulled back, and she looked to be in her early thirties. "Hello, Ms. Brazzell?" She said, unsure of how to pronounce my name. I nodded to assure her that she'd said it correctly. "How are you feeling?" She asked as if it weren't obvious. My hair piled messily on top of my head; my clothing was disheveled, the smell of puke resonating from my every breath. How the hell did she think I was feeling? I nodded as if to say just that sarcastically. "Well," she began, "you're not out of the woods yet. You scared your friend," She said, referring to Angela. "The doctors want me to interview you because they're recommending you be transferred to our psychiatric ward for evaluation." She said, trying to show concern looking for my reaction at the same time. I have none. I sat still as if I didn't hear what she'd said. "Ms. Brazzell?" She repeated. I looked up at her without saying a word. I didn't know why, but I was just exhausted and in no shape to refute anything she said. "So, maybe you can tell me a little about what caused you to be so upset." She inquired.

"I'd rather not." I snapped.

"Okay." She sighed as she turned on her heels and left the room.

"What is wrong with you?" Angela asked, both angry and confused. "If you don't start talkin', they're about to haul your ass off to Kings Wood! Is that what you want?" She warned.

I began to cry again. "No!" I sobbed.

"Well fucking act like it, then!" She angrily whispered. Just then, the tall lady returned to the room. Immediately, I began explaining my current situation as she penned what I was saying on a pad word for word.

After I told her of my ordeal, her eyes seemed to well up with tears. She struggled to keep her composure, but I could tell my story affected her. She then handed me a Styrofoam cup filled with a thick black liquid.

"What's this?" I asked, disgusted at the color and consistency of the liquid I held in my hand.

"It's liquid charcoal." She explained. "You have to drink it to absorb the remaining toxins in your stomach from the pills you ingested," she said. I sat there for a minute, thinking "no way in hell I'm going to let this shit touch my lips." "C'mon, drink up." She urged. I held my nose and forced it down in one gulp. I have still to this day never tasted anything so fucking horrible. The doctor left the room once more and returned shortly after that with discharge papers, a referral to a psychiatrist, and a piece of paper that read: May God grant me the serenity to accept the things I cannot change, change the things I can, and the wisdom to know the difference. It's called the serenity prayer, and its powerful words I still carry with me to this day.

Chapter 17

After coming so close to ending my own life, I left the hospital with a different outlook on life. Although I was still tremendously affected by the trauma I'd experienced, I realized that I could either let this cripple me for life or get back up and fight. I chose to fight. I immediately began searching for new employment, feeling that was the first step to taking my life back. My career was my independence, and my freedom was my life. I hated the idea of someone being able to ration out money to me or control what I could and couldn't do because I relied upon them. I began to pay close attention to my looks again. I started exercising, keeping my hair and nails done, and being well dressed as I had before. I found a new salon on Seven Mile Road and arranged a meeting with the manager. Yes, I was excited about getting back up.

Nicara was the manager of the new salon, called Shay's. Ironically enough, Shay's was not my salon, but I immediately felt at home. Nicara was abrasive when I first met her, but after we warmed up to one another, she was quite sweet. Nicara and I birthdays were two days apart, which made us both Libras. For this reason, I think we identified with one another more than either of us cared to admit. Nicara was a few years older than me, and over the next few years, I began to look up to her as a big sister. She was an exceptional hair stylist, and I admired her talent and skill. She specialized in short hair, and people lined up to sit in her chair. She was classy and exuded style and grace, qualities I found most Libras had. The thing I liked best about her was that she didn't have a "jealous" bone in her body. If there was something another stylist was good at, she always gave them their props and even threw them, clients. It was like she knew she was good and there was no need to cut the other stylists down. Instead, she built us all up. This was especially fulfilling to me because I had been hated on in every salon I'd worked in previously. No matter how polite I was to my counterparts, some jealous female always had to show her ass.

I'd settled in quite nicely at my new workspace and was getting along well with my new colleagues. Everyone welcomed me with open arms. They were warm, and it felt like a family. There was Nadia, a sweet girl, but so hood. She had four daughters and was your typical ghetto chick, but mad cool. Every day she came in with some colorful, hilarious story from her always eventful life. Her daughters ranged in age from ten months to ten years. She had twin babies who were ten months and two older girls. They were sweet kids, but in my opinion, at the salon far too often. The workplace is not a place for your children. Then, there was Tamia. She was quiet and very polite and kept to herself. Nadia rarely ever participated in the often-animated group discussions that took place at the shop. There was also Wayne. He was a young boy, fresh out of high school and apparently gay. He was very talented with hair. He had a lot of clients, mostly around his age. We also had a manicurist name Quia. She and I became very cool. She did the best pink and white set, which was how I liked to wear my nails. She had the cheeriest personality, and I loved that about her.

Chapter 18

Despite my new-found success professionally, my relationship with Angela never regained its momentum. We were just going through the motions, and our once-perfect little family had fallen apart. Myesha got wind of her mother's upcoming release from the treatment program and began to act out. Aside from pre-teen growing pains, being away from her mother had taken a toll on her. Though I believe she was grateful for Angela stepping in to rescue her, she was too young to understand what was best for her. Like any child, she just wanted her mother. She eventually went back to live with Jeanette and soon it was only Angela and me. I wanted her and me to make it and, although I couldn't put my finger on it, something between us was missing. Something just wasn't right. My womanly intuition convinced me that she was, at the very least, interested in someone else. Still, we pressed on and stayed together.

I began to try to find other things to occupy my mind. I'd recently decided to start singing again and sought out venues to do so. When I was on stage performing, it was the only time I felt free. When I was singing, it seemed as if all of the anger, all of the stress, and all of the fear left me. I felt invincible. I felt admired. I felt beautiful. People loved me and loved to hear my voice. My voice was the only thing in my life that I ever had total confidence in. My biological father was a singer, and before he began using crack, he could wow a crowd with his beautiful melodies. He was a talented songwriter and also played the drums. As a child, I enjoyed the stories of how he'd pull a chair onto the stage at gigs and take my pregnant mom's hand and place her in it. He'd serenade her and essentially, me, his unborn child. He used to say that by the time he was done, there wasn't a dry eye in the house. As I said before, the gift of song was the only good thing my father ever gave me. I could leave any audience in awe with my voice, and that was a fantastic feeling.

Around this time, drag shows were top-rated in the gay community. Surprisingly, there were not many opportunities for the real girls to perform at the gay venues, but I was determined to help change that. I happened to meet a very popular performer, who ultimately became my "gay mother." She was very well known for her off-the-chart stage shows. Her bright costumes and well put together performances made her an icon in the industry. Being one of DeAngela Show Shannon's children opened a lot of doors for me. I was invited to perform at all of the clubs and events around the city. I met lots of influential people and was embraced by the L.G.B.T. community. It felt like family. Soon, I was performing at different locations at least three times a week and was quickly making a name for myself.

One night, after my set, I was approached by a young lady. She introduced herself as Tesha, and by the seductive look in her eyes, I knew in my heart she would be trouble, but I still proceeded. The attraction between us was instant and with my current relationship on the rocks, I was an easy target. I tried to do the right thing, introducing Tesha to my girlfriend, almost using Angela as a shield from that "come hither" look that read all over Tesha's face. My attempts, however, were to no avail. As the following weeks progressed, I noticed that every club I performed in, Tesha would, coincidentally, show up. I began to "run into" her more and more, and she always made it a point to be seen. She seemed like cool people, and I thought that the three of us could hang out and maintain a platonic friendship. Me, my girlfriend, and her ex. Little did I know, Tesha had me in her crosshairs, and she had no intention of Angela being anywhere in the equation.

Soon, Tesha and I began to hang out alone, and though I was attracted to her, I did try to keep it strictly just friends. She had a boyfriend, and I had a girlfriend, and we needed to be on that level and nothing more. One night, I had a gig at The Rainbow Room, and since Angela didn't want to go, Tesha offered to drive me. The night at the club went much like any other. I completed my performance; we had a few drinks and decided to call it a night. We were headed west down

Eight Mile Road toward my house when, suddenly, Tesha pulled onto a side street just off of Mound Road. I wasn't sure why she did that, but by now I was feeling woozy from the effects of the drinks. She threw the car into park and unfastened her seatbelt. Without warning, she leaned in and kissed me on the lips. I sat there stunned. I couldn't believe this was happening. Though I was sure that my relationship was headed to the girlfriend graveyard, I still felt gut-wrenching guilt. I was becoming what I was most repulsed by, a cheater. Again, I couldn't fight this magnetic attraction to this girl. There was something about her, and I was no match for whatever it was. I was already lonely and sexually deprived, seeing as though my girlfriend all but ignored me. Even more tempting, Tesha was a femme, the total opposite of Angela.

When I didn't resist, she kissed me again. I started to feel something familiar…Something I hadn't felt in quite some time. She started kissing me again and with more and more intensity, and I didn't even bother to argue. By now, my panties were wet, and we were going at it full force. We kept kissing and soon our hands were all over each other. I could feel her chiseled body, and she had the softest ass. By now, my shirt was down around my waist, and my breasts were exposed. She sucked and squeezed them, and this sent me into a frenzy. The fact that I hadn't been with a femme lesbian in so long was turning me on even more, and I suddenly felt the need to dominate her. I shoved her back down into the driver seat, and the look on her face read both surprise and confusion. Just as she was about to ask what was wrong, I was on top of her. I reached down on the side of the seat and pulled the lever to let the seat back. I tore at her pants and managed to get them down around her ankles. I put my face between her legs and began to let her have it. I was licking and sucking, the adrenaline of her voice singing out, made me please her more. "Yeah...oh...don't stop..." She repeated. Her clit tasted so damn delicious. Immediately I knew I would have no problem eating pussy. I was hooked. I loved the taste and the smell. I knew how to do it well because I knew how I liked it done to me. I licked and sucked, keeping my tongue wet. I felt her tense up, and I knew what would come next. Splash! I felt the creamiest shower all over my lips, and it was so good. Suddenly, I began to feel the heaviest feeling in my heart. What had I just done? Even though I had my suspicions of what Angela was doing while my back was turned, I had no proof, and also If I did, did that make what I did right? I felt like shit! Now I'd have to go and lay next to my woman with another woman's pussy on my tongue. I needed my ass whipped!

I got home, and as I got ready to go to bed, I felt tremendous guilt. I crawled into bed and contrary to what had been going on for months, Angela snuggled close to me. All of a sudden, she wanted to cuddle? Be close to me? Kiss me even? I was stunned. She'd acted like I wasn't even there for months and now that I was officially fucking someone else, she wanted me? Wow! As guilty as I felt, I couldn't help but feel a sense of accomplishment. Is this what I had to do to get my point across? Though

I had gotten the attention that I'd longed for the past three months, I couldn't help but feel a sinking feeling in my stomach. I was pretty sure from her actions that Angela was unfaithful, I felt so guilty for cheating on her. I did care for her. She'd told me of her past relationships, where people had done her wrong and cheated on her, and I was horrified to think that I was now one of those people.

Chapter 19

For the next few months, Tesha and I continued to see each other. I'd even managed to incorporate her into our lives. She hung out with Angela and me and played the friend role perfectly. This made me feel bad at first, but I somehow began to justify my actions in my mind. I started to feel like I was right because I'd initially thought that she was victimizing me. I felt that Angela was doing her thing on the side, so what was right for her was right for me.

One particular night, I was upset with Angela, and it was my birthday weekend. She was so nonchalant about it. I felt as if she'd forgotten. It was like she hadn't even planned on celebrating my birthday at all. I was disgusted. The honoring of birthdays has always been a big deal to me and is to this day. Whenever her birthday came around, I made her feel like "the man." She and I shared the same birthday month, but I always made it a point to make her think it was all about her. I was so upset about her failure to acknowledge my day and when Tesha got wind of this that was her window of opportunity. She immediately picked me up from my house. After taking me shopping and buying me some charming things, she took me to her home. By this time, she'd split up with her boyfriend and was living single. After making me a fabulous dinner by candlelight, she had a specific plan for what she wanted to do next. She led me to her bedroom. She went to her armoire and drew open one of the doors. She pulled a black bag reached into the pocket and pulled out, at first, what looked to be a belt. Upon closer inspection, I could see that this belt held a little something extra…a cock. It was an eight-inch jelly cock, bright in color, with balls and attached to nylon strap harness. She handed it to me, and I was like a kid in a candy store. Angela had been the only one who'd used a strap-on with me, and she'd never let me do her. Angela was very conservative when it came to sex, at least with me. Angela didn't want me to touch her breasts, put my fingers in her and don't even ask to wear the strap and fuck her. I tried for two plus years to get Angela to be more adventurous, all to no avail.

When Tesha handed me the strap, I jumped at the chance. It was apparent that I excited. With no hesitation, had the strap-on around my waist. I began by eating her out. I always liked to get her wet before we got all the way into it. After she was climbing the headboard, I eased up on top of her. I kissed her lips softly, brushing her hair from her face. I felt a combination of happiness, horniness, euphoria, and fear all at the same time. I took the cock into my hands and guided it toward her vaginal opening. I felt it hit her body and I took a deep breath. I put it in her slow, and I swear I could feel her warmth wrapped around me. I sighed, feeling like I'd just submerged myself in warm bath water. I began to thrust, really slowly at first, being careful not to hurt her. If there was one thing I knew by having one of my own, it was that pussy was a very delicate thing. She began to move in rhythm with me, and that let me know that she was enjoying it. Her legs were wrapped around me, almost pushing me into her. She moaned, and so did I. It felt so good to be inside her like the dick was actually mine. How could this be true? How could it feel like this prosthetic penis was anatomically attached to me and I was inside this pussy for real? I thrust deeper inside of her and then I exploded. I swear if I could secrete sperm, Tesha would've been pregnant with quintuplets at that moment. I enjoyed the experience of giving head and while being penetrated; but penetrating a woman felt so amazing! This feeling was one that was so unfamiliar, so different, and so good. It was purely mental. It was one that was fueled exclusively by intellectual stimulation. Imagination was a compelling thing, and for the first time, I knew it.

I wasn't a smoker, but I knew how the people in the movies felt when they needed a cigarette after sex. I'd never felt such intense sexual pleasure with any man, ever. There was just no comparison. The bonus, as if it could get any better, was the emotional aspect. It's a common misconception that a lesbian connection is purely sexual and that couldn't be further from the truth. The sexual tension is just a plus to the many other things that make up lesbian relationships. It's just another perk of having a healthy female relationship. We lay in her bed and held each other until we drifted off to sleep. In what seemed like record time, I was awakened by a warm feeling on my face. My eyes opened and met the glare of the sun shining through her window. I said aloud "Oh my god!" startling Tesha. "I have to go...Oh my god!" I repeated frantically. In two years, I'd never been so disrespectful to my woman as to spend the night away from home. Even though we were beefed out, I still had an obligation to be home by a specific time of night because we were still, technically, a couple. I was panicked as I dressed and prepared to go home. Tesha hopped up and dressed, and we headed out the door. I shuttered at the thought of what might happen when I got back. Angela didn't get angry often, but when she did, it was severe.

We pulled in front of my building, and I wasn't sure what to expect. I waved bye to my mistress and headed inside. I started up the stairs and walked as slow as I could down the corridor. I reached the apartment door and hesitated. I wouldn't have been surprised if the locks had been changed. I'd checked my cell, and it read ten missed calls...all from Angela. I inserted my key and opened the door. I reluctantly went inside and was surprised to find the apartment empty. I breathed a sigh of relief. I put my purse down and began to undress. I headed for the shower and hopped in. After trying in vain to wash away the guilt, I threw on something comfortable and lay in the bed. I was beginning to get exhausted with the lies and things I was doing to keep my relationship with Tesha a secret, while my real relationship hung by a thread. Tears came to my eyes because I was so unhappy but unsure of what to do. On the one hand, I'd become accustomed to the stability that my relationship with Angela afforded me, but the lack of physical and emotional connection ate at me. It made me feel inadequate. I really couldn't handle the feeling of not being good enough. I knew I wasn't perfect, but up to this point, I had tried to be the best woman I could be to Angela, and my efforts seemed to go unnoticed. As my thoughts began to run away with me, I heard keys at the front door. Oh, my God! Angela was home. I snuggled underneath the covers and pretended to be asleep. I wished I could just disappear. I heard her enter the room and I was as nervous as a hooker in church. The pounding in my chest began to pound fast and hard. I could hear her hanging her coat in the closet and putting down her things. I suddenly felt the bed depress beside me. She lay down and then shifted toward me. My back was to her, so she pulled the covers back, exposing my head. I felt her lips kiss my cheek and I got even more nervous. Was she kissing me goodbye before she killed me? I was confused and scared. She reached over my shoulder, and in her hand was a small red box. I didn't know whether she knew I was awake or not, so I hesitated before putting on an Oscar-deserving performance.

I yawned and said in the sleepiest voice, "Hey Bay...when you get here?" I turned to her, and I'm sure the confusion resonated on my face. I stared at the box she held in her hand.

She said, "Happy Birthday!" I was astonished not to hear the slightest amount of anger in her voice. She lifted the top from the box, and I couldn't believe my eyes. My mouth fell open in disbelief. "Will you marry me?" She asked. I sat there frozen and in shock. In the box was a white gold ring with beautiful princess cut diamonds. I was speechless. Now I felt like the scum of the earth. Maybe I'd been wrong about her. Perhaps I'd just been a selfish bitch. How could I have been carrying on this affair and all along my woman was contemplating marriage? She wanted to wife me, and I was fucking around on her. I was so ashamed, and, at that moment, I knew this thing with Tesha, and I had to stop!

"Yes! Yes! Baby! Yes!" I exclaimed as I hugged and kissed my woman more passionately than I had in months. I'd been proposed to by men, but this was different. I could see myself walking down the aisle in all white and becoming one with a woman...this woman.

Chapter 20

For the first few weeks of our engagement, things were great between Angela and me. It was almost like when we'd first met. We were going on dates, wining and dining and the sex was hot. I'd officially broken things off with Tesha, and she was not happy about it. I felt terrible for her having become a casualty as a result of my frivolousness, but I had to do it if Angela and I were going to be married. In retrospect, I was so young and hadn't grasped the full concept of what marriage was. At the time, I think I was more in love with the idea of being married. I say this because, though I'd accepted a ring, my mind never really went to the extent of actually being a wife or what changes that would bring about. And still, I wanted to embrace my new role as the fiancé. Angela had become somewhat suspicious of Tesha and our friendship and expressed that she was uncomfortable with us hanging out together. I reassured her it was over, and we wouldn't see each other again. I couldn't bring myself to admit to the despicable acts I'd been engaging in with her. I felt so guilty, yet my selfishness wouldn't allow me to give my fiancé what she so deserved…the truth.

Angela and I were enjoying our newfound pre-marital bliss. I wasn't sure what sparked Angela's sudden change of heart, however, one minute, I was invisible to her and the next she was so all in. I didn't know what caused the change, but I loved the attention. Maybe the underlying threat of someone taking her place made her think twice. Little did she know, Tesha could never have replaced her. Tesha was sweet, kind, and fun to be with, but she had a promiscuous side, and I could have never taken her seriously in a relationship. There was just something about her that I didn't trust, coupled with the fact that she still had an insatiable appetite for the male persuasion, certainly something I was not prepared to tolerate.

One particular night, I left work and hurried home, fully expecting my woman to greet me. To my surprise, I came home to an empty apartment. Initially, I figured she'd gone out to the store or on an errand, but three hours and two voicemail messages later; my emotions went from wonder, to worry, to anger. I figured if that was the case, she should at least call me and tell me she was okay. Three more hours passed and now I was furious. I paced the floor and attempted to watch TV to calm my nerves. Just when I could feel steam rising from the top of my head, I could hear keys in the front door. The door swung open, and Angela damn near fell in. She was uncontrollably drunk, stumbling all over the place. I could smell the cognac coming from her pores. I reached for her arm, but before I could get a word out, she took one look at me and blurted out "You're a lying', cheating,' dirty bitch!" I was floored!

I couldn't believe my ears. She never talked to me this way, and we didn't even play that "bitch" shit. "Excuse me?!" I growled.

"You've been fucking that bitch all along!" She continued. "Tell me the fucking truth RIGHT NOW!" She demanded. I hung my head in shame. I wasn't sure what had taken place before she came home, or why she picked now to confront me.

"Yes. I did" I muttered.

"You did what?! What exactly did you do?" She inquired. A few moments of awkward silence passed before I finally managed to say, "I slept with Tesha and I am sorry" I began to cry. I was sorry. I didn't want to hurt anyone, especially Angela. I cared about her and how she felt. How could I betray her like that? Was it worth it? I had no idea, yet, but I would soon meet another bitch...Karma.

Angela wasted no time ripping me a new one. She called me everything, but a child of God and I just took it, because I knew I was wrong. By the time she was finished sounding off, it was clear that she didn't want me around, in my mind at least. I was so humiliated and broken down that I couldn't even look Angela in the face. Although she didn't say it, she wanted me to leave, and I felt at that moment, that I should. I threw a few things in a bag and headed for the door. My stubborn attitude wouldn't dare allow me to take the car that Angela had bought for me. I reached the bottom of the stairwell at the front of the building and called the only person I could think of, Tesha.

Tesha pulled in front of the building in what seemed like no time and helped me load my bag into her car. We drove to her place in silence. I did not want to relive what had taken place moments earlier. I think Tesha subconsciously felt vindicated that she had been given a second chance to move in on me. She had been clear to me that she did not want what we had to end and now that it seemed my relationship was over, she felt confident that she would be my next prospect. Over the next couple of days, I spent my time contemplating my next move, while Tesha contemplated our future together. Aside from the fact that I still wanted Angela, I was quite suspicious of Tesha. She was just way too friendly and flirtatious...especially with men. Since I'd been with Angela, I was entirely off men and had never felt better, so right then, and I decided I would never compete with a man for a woman's affection. I wanted a woman who wanted what I could be to her...a woman. If a man was what she wanted from time to time, I wasn't about to be on standby, waiting for her to finish each tryst. I was worthy of being the only one in my mate's world. Ironically, I realized that the same was true of Angela. She was worthy of being the only one in my world. She deserved my devotion and undivided attention. I decided then that, that was precisely what she'd get.

Chapter 21

Truthfully, I missed Angela, and I didn't want anyone else. I enjoyed the familiarity of our relationship. I knew I had become complacent and used to her and it hurt to feel that slipping away. After some time apart and after a lot of pleading and prodding, Angela was finally persuaded to give our relationship another chance. I had all but begged her to give me another shot to prove to her that I could be faithful...that I could be the woman, she needed me to be. Over the next several months, I did put forth a serious effort to do precisely that. By this time, the summer was coming around, and I'd reconnected with my old friend Janeen. Her marriage to the prick had dissolved entirely by now, and the woman she'd left him for was no longer in the picture either. Janeen may not have been book smart, but she undoubtedly possessed street intelligence. She had mad game, and she was good at reeling people in with that sexy Caribbean accent. She had no problem getting a man or a woman to take her in and support her completely. She was the kind of woman who liked to be kept. She never really held a steady job but was always well-dressed and put together. She could barely read but was so good at the "gift of gab," she had everyone convinced that there was some language barrier to blame, but I knew that English was, indeed, the primary language among Trinidadians. Still, everyone doted on the charming foreigner, and unbeknownst to me, my own woman was no exception. I considered Janeen, a good friend. We hung out together and always had a fantastic time. She was a barrel of laughs, and so was I. We drank, talked shit, ate, shopped, and worked together. She was kind of like a slightly older sister, though she was technically old enough to be my mother. Janeen had a youthful spirit and loved to have fun. I loved her, but not for the same reasons that others did. She was never my idea of physically attractive. She wasn't ugly, but she wasn't the sort of woman I'd be attracted to. I could, however, see how others would have fallen victim to her little spell. She was charming and street smart and could her way out of or into anything. But, with all this charm and wit came a very shady side. Janeen was a woman who got what she wanted and was willing to step on anyone to make it happen.

Janeen was now coming around on a regular basis and hanging out with Angela and me. I was always told never to trust someone you think is your friend around your significant other but being that I never really had it in me to be jealous or insecure in that department, I paid their "innocent" flirting no mind. Little did I know, Janeen wanted what I had, and had every intention of getting what she wanted. She and Ben had split for good, and she was on the prowl for her next host. I was naïve to the fact that, like most people Janeen came across, Angela was engrossed in her little trance. Coupled with their little crush on one another, Angela never really forgave me for cheating on her, and she'd use this as the perfect opportunity to seek the ultimate revenge.

By now, things were banging at the salon, and I was swamped with satisfied customers. Money wasn't a thing, and Angela and I were doing quite well. We went out to eat, shopped and went to the clubs regularly, but still, something was off. I couldn't quite put my finger on it, but something was missing in our relationship. After the whole "Tesha" episode, things were just never quite the same. I wanted things to be normal again, but we just couldn't get it back. The sex was almost never by now, and we were both drinking heavily. I was determined to "fix" this relationship and was swimming deep in the river of denial. I was convinced that things would get better.

One particular night, Janeen and two of her acquaintances had come to the apartment to have a drink with Angela and me. We had gotten the jump on them and had already started drinking before they arrived. We were sipping our Hennessy and Cranberry Juice when they knocked at the door.

Janeen shouted "What's up my niggas" enthusiastically in her thick accent as she entered the apartment. Before I could answer, she made a bee-line for the kitchen and declared "Let me mix the drinks!" The excitement in her voice suggested that she was in good spirits. She'd brought along John and another girl that called herself Zena, but I don't think that was her real name. The name was fake, I was sure of it, and everything else screamed FAKE to me, which made me never care for her. She was the typical "stereotype" of what society concerned to be "pretty," and she knew it! But deep inside I knew she was insecure by her actions. She would make herself available to anyone interested. You know the type. Pretty with no substance.

Janeen mixed drinks for the three of them, and everyone took a seat in the living room in front of the TV. We engaged in small talk, all the while, gulping down drinks. Before long, we were tipsy, talking trash, and laughing hysterically. Janeen and I played the dozens all the time, and the alcohol just intensified it that much more. Janeen was a show-off in every sense of the word, and the fact that she had an audience to impress, two of which she'd already slept with, made her relentless. Others were an easy target for Janeen's sharp tongue, but I had a sword of my own beyond my lips. We went back and forth in playful argument, and then I said something for which Janeen had no comeback. Everyone was now laughing at her expense. She decided she'd try a different approach. She suddenly retorted "Tiny...Control your BITCH!"

A little stunned, but way too fueled by the alcohol, I barked "BITCH?!...I got your BITCH!" Shit just got real. What was once a funny conversation had been given a violent shove that turned serious. I felt as if I knew Janeen well enough to distinguish harmless teasing from outright disrespect...and this was disrespect. I wasn't at the point of wanting to fight just then, but I was passed an innocent cap session. She mumbled a few other obscenities until she said something audible.

"Low class, ghetto bitch..." she was saying as I caught the tail end of the sentence. I pondered in my mind for a second, whether or not this ignorant bitch just called me ghetto?

I convinced myself that she had. I rose to my feet and demanded: "Get the fuck out!" By this time, John was on his feet in an attempt to usher the two women to the front door. He did this to no avail as Janeen protested.

"I'm not going no motherfucking where! Tiny didn't say I had to leave!" She declared. Did this bitch just disregard what I said in MY house? Is she crazy? And did she just say MY woman's name like only HER opinion mattered?! Sure, this time, that I had heard her correctly before I could give it a second thought, I was across the coffee table with my hands clasped tightly around Janeen's throat. She pawed at John to release her, so she could get to me. Zena joined the struggle in an attempt to pry me off. As John and Zena tried to free Janeen from my firm grasp, the four of us moved toward the door in mid-scuffle. By now I was swinging my fists upon Janeen and was so enraged that I didn't know if the blows all landed on her or the others entangled in the brawl.

Finally, they exited the apartment, and while I was still in earshot, I could hear Zena questioning Janeen, "Did she hit you?" I heard her inquire in a huffy voice. I then trained my attention on Zena.

I exploded through the screen door of the apartment. "And if I did, BITCH?" I retorted. "What the fuck are you going to do if I did hit her,

BITCH?" I demanded. Zena stood there like a deer in headlights. It was clear that she was surprised I'd overheard the conversation. An argument ensued between Zena and me. I could faintly hear John pleading with both women to leave with him and Janeen's drunken rants of slurred and inaudible obscenities.

By this time, Angela had come onto the balcony and was yelling obscenities as well. It was only when she tugged at my arm that I realized her anger was directed at me. She screamed, cursed, and snatched at my clothing angrily. My confusion kept me from making out her words. "Stupid ho, drunk bitch" Was all I heard. Was she talking to me when I had been so blatantly disrespected in our home? She was. She was taking that bitch's side. Wow! At that point, my anger turned to rage.

"Get the fuck off me!" I demanded as I jerked myself from her grip. Before I knew it, she and I were in a violent struggle. I was swinging wildly, sure now that my blows were landing upon her. In one swift motion, she pushed me with such force that I felt my face slam hard into the bathroom door jam. I fell to the floor with the breath knocked clear out of me. I was dizzy and seeing stars when I felt a wet trickle rolling down the side of my jaw. I reached up and touched my lip. It felt mushy, like ground beef. I struggled to my feet and stumbled to the bathroom vanity mirror. My upper lip had a split of about three-quarters of an inch in its corner and was bleeding profusely. My rage went from sixty to a hundred at the sight of the gaping gash in my face. I needed stitches, but all I could think of was how I was going to fuck this bitch up who'd taken the side of the illiterate snake in the grass called Janeen and had in-turn, split my shit wide open. I charged out of the bathroom like a mad woman, still bleeding like a stuck pig. I reached the end of the hall when I heard male voices. I peered around the corner to the front door. Two police officers were standing in the doorway on the inside of the apartment. The tall black officer, who looked to be in his early thirties, was taking Angela's account of what had occurred as he jotted the details onto a small pad. I stood in the hallway and eavesdropped for a moment.

"She's been drinking. We had friends over, and she probably had a little bit too much to drink and got angrily drunk. I was able to calm her down so everything's under control and the other guests are gone." Angela explained to the Officers. The older white officer, short and rather stout, suggested that they take a look around to *"make sure what she's saying is right,"* as he put it. I then turned on my heels and tip-toed to the bedroom. I could hear the footsteps of the officers coming down the hall as I cowered in the corner alongside the bed. I listened to the door swing open, and soon a flashlight shone upon me. The black officer stood over me, Maglite in hand.

"Hey, …what's your name?" He said in a stern tone. Before I could answer, he asked again, "HEY!" He demanded, this time with more bass in his voice. It was no secret that I hated cops, so I decided at that point, if he were going to keep yelling at me like a jackass, then I would ignore him like the jackass he was.

I then stared up at him with a look that said, "What the hell are you yelling for, dumbass." He then lifted his foot and nudged my leg with it. At that point, I lost it.

"I know the fuck you didn't just put your mother fucking foot on me!" I exploded. With one hand he yanked me to my feet by my shirt. He threw me, face down, onto the bed. At that point, the fat white officer had come into the room and, while the black one practically ripped my arms from their joints to restrain me, held my hands at the small of my back and clasped the handcuffs tightly around my wrists. I don't recall being given my Miranda rights, as I was now crying hysterically and cursing the police officers at the same time. I was then escorted out of the apartment, down the wooden balcony and out of the glass entry doors to the complex. The cold, hard plastic of the seat in the back of the squad car was a harsh reality as I rode in silence to the eighth precinct where I'd spend the night and much of the next day. I'd amused myself by listening to my drunken cellmates rants all night long.

I finally heard a loud clang at the front of the cell. "Brazzell step up!" The burly, masculine female guard called out to me in a heavy voice. I leaped to my feet and ran to the exit. As I walked out of the gate, I spotted Angela in the hallway, clipboard in hand, signing some papers. The officer behind a thick fiberglass partition indicated that we were *"all set."*

Without even looking at me, Angela turned and walked past me toward the exit. I followed in silence. I was pissed at her, still, from the night before and couldn't wait to start in on her ass again, once we were out of the watchful eye of the police. I was livid that I'd spent the night in jail and rationalized with myself, it was this bitch's fault. She'd let this island whore disrespect me, and what's worse, she'd taken her side. I felt strength building in my *"slap-a-bitch"* arm.

"So, are you fucking that bitch or what?" I demanded. She grinned with her eyes trained on the road. This infuriated me. She formed her lips to respond, but before she could, I took the juice bottle from the cup holder in the center console and threw its content at her, making a loud splash all over her and the driver side window. Before she had a chance to retaliate, I was out of my seat and over into hers, twenty-piecing her with both fists. She struggled to steer the car with one hand, while trying, to no avail, to restrain me with her other. She finally jerked the steering wheel to the right abruptly swerving the car to the side of the road. She threw the gear shifter into park and quickly grasped my wrists with both hands. She shoved me; both of my wrists still tightly constricted by her hands and held me against the passenger door. I was ballistic by this time and struggling fiercely to get her to release me. I got one wrist free and with an open hand, began hitting her on her face, neck, forearms and wherever else my hand landed. She finally gave up trying to hold me down and as soon as I was ready to calm down, she slapped me across the face. Enraged, I reached up and dug my nails into the skin on her cheeks and pulled downward. Blood began to trickle down the sides of her face and onto the white Sean John T-shirt she wore. She was still on top of me hitting me anywhere she could when I pressed my right foot to her chest and pushed her off of me. In one motion I was back on top of her, swinging like a mad woman. By now, my shirt and bra were torn and hung off of me. Suddenly, I just stopped and retreated. The feeling of tremendous guilt overcame me as the realization that this was, after all, the woman I loved, came to mind. I looked down at her, and she was crying. I instantly felt like a stake had been driven through my heart. I retreated to the passenger seat, feeling as low as low could get. She lay slumped over, almost in a fetal position, in the driver's seat for what seemed like hours...weeping. I knew then that this was the beginning of the end.

Chapter 22

"Hello...you've reached Sherae. Sorry, I can't take your call right now but leave a message, and I'll get back to you." Beep! I heard on the other end of the phone.

"Rae, this is Shae. I need to talk to you. Hit me up alright?" I spoke back to the voicemail that had so cheerfully greeted me. Rae was a great friend of mine. She and I had met through Janeen, an unlikely source, since most of the superficial, fake as an eight- dollar bill, bitches Janeen hung with I couldn't stand. But Rae was cool as hell and not one fake bone in her body. Rae was a dancer she was fine. She had golden, smooth skin, big brown eyes, and a pretty smile. She had a slender build and stood about 5'5" with the perfect breast I'd ever seen. Her ass was equally perfect, and if you sat your drink on it, she could carry it without spilling it. Her personality was as beautiful as her exterior. She was so kind and down to earth, unlike a lot of girls as pretty as her. Since she and I were close, she was the perfect one to ask this favor.

About an hour passed and then I heard my cell phone ring. "Hello?" I inquired.

Rae cheerfully replied, "Hi, sexy!" "What's up?" She continued. "It's a long story, but the short version is Tiny, and I broke it off, and I don't want to stay in that apartment with her."

I told her. "You know I have a spare room." She offered.

"C'mon, Corrine won't mind..." She assured me. Corrine was Sharae's girlfriend. Like Rae, Corrine was beautiful. She was a light-skinned stud with butter-smooth skin and curly jet-black hair that she wore in a Caesar with 360○ waves that could make you sick. She had a perfect, pearly white smile and could charm any woman, gay or straight, right out of their panties. She was smooth as silk, and she knew it. Corrine had a dark side though. As sweet as Sharae was, I couldn't figure out for the life of me why Corrine treated her the way she did. She was verbally abusive and fucking everything that moved while sweet Sharae watched in horror. Rae was so in love with Corrine that, for the longest, she just sat back and took whatever this girl dished out. I felt bad. Though over the few years I'd known them, I'd befriended Corrine as well; I couldn't help but be a little salty at her for dogging my girl the way she did. What was weird was that Sharae seemed so happy with Corrine. Even with all her cheating and such, Rae didn't seem to want to end the relationship. Unbeknownst to me, Rae had devised a plan to appease her woman's appetite for side dishes.

One rainy November night I'd stopped by the grocery store on the way home. After settling into my room, in the apartment I now shared with my friends, I took a break from unpacking and went to the kitchen to prepare a meal as a token of my appreciation. Since Rae didn't cook much and their diet pretty much consisted of Taco Bell and McDonald's, I felt this home-cooked meal would be well received. I'd decided on Chicken Alfredo since I knew it was Corrine's favorite. I drained the cooked pasta and set it to the side while I prepared the crème sauce. Parmesan cheese, heavy crème, and voila! I tossed the noodles, sauce, and chicken together in a large pot and removed the garlic bread from the oven. I have to say; I'm a bad, bad bitch in the kitchen! I bet the people are driving down Eight Mile Road could smell that good cooking. Dinner was served, but I had no idea what they'd had in mind for dessert. After dinner, the three of us sat down at the small square shaped dinette set in the dining area of the apartment. As we ate, we exchanged small talk about the events of the day and they each complimented me on how good the chicken Alfredo was. After we'd had our fill, I cleared the plates from the table and stacked them in the sink. I then took my place at the table where we continued to engage in conversation. I described to them how my relationship had finally ended and they each gave their take on the situation as outsiders looking in.

In the midst of the conversation, Rae left the table and retreated to her bedroom. She was gone a few minutes and then re-emerged with a large bottled of clear tequila. "Let's play a game and do shots, "She cheerfully suggested. I was an avid tequila drinker, but never had the pleasure of trying the clear one. I'd always enjoyed the gold, but I would abruptly learn the difference. By the third time out on the question game, answering a question with an actual answer bought me a one-way ticket to a drunken stupor. I could drink gold tequila with the best of them, but this "white girl" Rae introduced me to had me FUCKED UP! I was tipsy, and I guess it is evident because I was now the butt of Rae and Corrine's drunken jokes. I managed to get to my feet, just barely, and stumble to my room. I shut the door behind me, leaving Corrine and Rae in the dining room, still giggling at my inebriated antics. I began to strip once alone in my room because for some reason I was, all of a sudden, burning up. I was in a cold sweat. I got my clothes off and melted into the pallet I'd made for myself on the floor. No sooner than my head hit the pillow, I began to drift off. I was almost comatose when I saw a light come through a cracked door. I wasn't sure if I was dreaming or not when I saw two silhouettes go into the room. I didn't budge, as I was sure this was a mirage, and I was too drunk to try to figure it out at this point. The dark images moved closer to me, and both knelt down beside me. I could only watch their every action as my drunken state rendered me temporarily paralyzed. I watched as the two bodies entangled each other, and I soon realized that they were naked and making out. I wasn't sure what was going on, but I was intrigued. I watched as they kissed and caressed each other. By now, I'd snapped back to reality and realized that the two dark images were indeed my roommates. I was still too out of it to speak, but now this make-out session had my full and undivided attention. The taller, curvier body, now identified as Rae, climbed onto Corrine and began to bounce up and down. The light that shone through the crack in the bedroom door now allowed me to see that Corrine was indeed wearing a strap. Was this happening in my room and front of me?

Still frozen in my drunken daze, I felt hands on my breasts. I wasn't sure whose they were, but I did know they were coming from the knot of flesh beside me. Then I felt lips and a wet tongue encircling my left nipple. This took me by surprise. All the years I'd been friends with them, it had never occurred to me that they saw me in this light. I tried to push the hands and mouth of my would-be seductress, now identified as Rae, away. I was feeling so awkward. After all, this was a dear friend, and I happened to know that friendship and sex rarely mix. Still, she persisted, and at this point, I was in no position to resist. After giving my breast a proper tongue lashing, Rae suddenly stopped and moved aside. I wondered what made her do so and just as I caught myself about to ask, a warm presence hovered above me. I felt the phallus enter me and I cried out. The cry was one of both pleasure and shock. Corrine began to thrust deeper until I could feel her pelvic bone against mine. Rae seemed to fade into the background as Corrine pounded me harder. It felt so good. I cried repeatedly. I came in multiples at the thrusting of Corrine's cock. I could feel her dark body over me as she climaxed. She rolled onto the side of me where she collapsed, panting and sweating. In one quick motion, Rae straddled Corrine and was back riding her. The light through the cracked door allowed me to see Rae's perfect ass cheeks bouncing up and down on Corrine's dick. I was in a state of both shock and sexual bliss. I heard Corrine's voice cry out in a guttural moan. She'd climaxed while Rae rode her. Rae climbed off of her and lay on the floor next to her. I was still in disbelief.

Chapter 23

The next morning, I awoke to find myself alone in my room. Consciously, I knew that what had taken place hadn't been some super-erotic dream, but for the sake of my sense of decency, I wanted to believe it was. I snatched the covers over my head and peered underneath and was shocked to see my own naked body. I rushed to my feet and threw on my boy shorts and a wife-beater and exited the bedroom. I walked cautiously around the apartment, peeking into every room, but found that I was alone. Rae and Corrine had gone about the day, and all I could think was how awkward it was going to be when they returned. I raced back to my room, gathered my towel and toiletries and headed for the shower. I wanted to get ready and leave before they got back, and I had to face the reality of what had transpired the night before. I quickly dressed and left the apartment, locking the heavy door behind me. I headed down the stairwell and into the elongated parking lot. I often forgot where I parked, but this time I'd nearly surveyed the entire log and couldn't find my car. Could this be happening? Had my car been stolen? I'd been smart and invested in an anti-theft device, called the "Club," and had used it religiously and the night before had been no exception. Could a thief take the car with the device on it? All these thoughts flooded my mind, and just as I started to panic, a light bulb went off: who had the spare key to both my car and the club? Angela.

My state of shock and panic quickly turned to anger as I furiously punched the keys on my cell phone and dialed Angela's number. The other end rang in my ear. "You've reached Tiny, leave a message." Her voicemail greeting cheerfully sang. I angrily depressed the "end" key and hung up. I quickly redialed her. This time, there was no ring, just went straight to voicemail. I shouted in frustration. An on-looking man stared and snickered as I threw my mini-tantrum in the parking lot. I gave him the dirtiest look I could muster, and he quickly retreated to his car. I paced back and forth for a second and contemplated what I'd do next. Finally, I searched my cell's phone book to find Rae's number. I pressed the send button and waited for her to pick up. Once she did, I gave her the short version of what happened, and in no time, was there to get me.

The ride was smooth but long as we made our way to my place of work. The salon was busy, and everyone seemed to be in a good mood except me. I was furious that this bitch that was apparently fucking my friend dared to come and be a fucking Indian-giver. She had bought that car for ME. She had no right to take it back. The salon wasn't far from the apartment I once shared with Angela. I had a right mind to call a cab, get in it and go bust out every window and flatten the tires on the damn car. If she were going to take it back, then it would be of no use to her silly ass. Just as I was seriously contemplating this devious deed, my cell phone rang.

"Hello!" I spat into the phone angrily, not even bothering first to check the call I.D.

"Dang, Ma. Why you sound all mean and shit?" A buttery smooth voice serenaded into my ear.

"Corrine?" I inquired. She continued to smooth-talk.

"What's up, boo?" I asked, still feeling awkward at being their third wheel.

"Are you coming straight home tonight?" She quizzed. I cautiously answered, "I think so," not knowing where this was going.

"Good!" I have someone that wants to meet you "she said.

"OK." I simply replied.

"C U later." She replied, and then hung up. I wondered for the rest of the day who it could be that wanted to meet me.

About a month before I moved in with Rae and Corrine, I'd been a participant in our city's hair awards. It's very popular show where the city's top hair designers come together and showcase their talent. Models, props, designers, and entertainment as far as the eye can see. I had gotten a room at the host hotel and made a weekend of it. I had four models: Rae; Dashawn; Tara; and Sapphire. We all had a good old fashion slumber party at the hotel and had a blast modeling at the hair show. Apparently, I caught the attention of a certain someone at the show, with my intricate routine and fierce hand-made-by-me-outfits. I was a bad bitch when it came to production, theatre, dance, and entertainment. My models executed the routine perfectly and modeled my hair with perfection, leaving the entire crowd in awe. There were a lot of things I wasn't, but when it came to the hair game, I was flawless.

The certain someone was Corrine's boss Brenda. She managed the car detailing facility that Corrine worked at. Brenda was as smooth as Corrine. She was short about 5'2", light-brown skinned, slim, with mesmerizing brown eyes, and the cutest laugh. Brenda dressed like a teenage boy and was neat and clean-cut. The fact that she had a good job and things going for her made her even more attractive. However, I was told, Brenda had a live-in girlfriend. Did she expect to meet and kick it with me and continue being in a relationship with someone else? Hell no. I wasn't having that…or was I? I got home that evening and exited the taxi in front of the apartment building. I started up the stairs toward the apartment and fished for my keys. I opened the door and as I stepped in, caught a glimpse of Brenda standing in the doorway of Rae and Corrine's room. Corrine heard me come in and motioned for me to go into her room. I did so, and as I walked past Brenda, caught a whiff of the sweetest smelling cologne. I swear I became wet at the smell. She drank in the sight of me, slowly looking me up and down, as I caught her in my peripheral vision.

"Brenda wants to hear you sing." Corrine began. "I told her how awesome you were." She continued. If I'd been white, I'd have turned beet red. I'd never been much for being suddenly put on the spot. I laughed nervously and frantically searched my brain for a clever response. Finally, I said

"Right here, right now? I laughed nervously.

"Yes!" She quizzed. I could see that she was not going to let me off the hook.

"I don't even know..." I managed to say before Corrine cut me off. Sing Alicia Keys. She requested. I took a deep breath and realized I was as nervous as a whore in church. "Baby, baby," I began to belt out. Through half closed eyes, I could see a look of both shock and pleasure pasted on Brenda's face. I knew I had her...

"I want to book you for our upcoming show at Bert's on Broadway," Brenda interrupted.

"Ok, sure..." I responded without hesitation. She gave me the details about the show, and I gave her my contact information and my rate of pay, though little did she know, she could've had me for free...

Over the next few days, I gathered my wardrobe and music for my upcoming performance and practiced my songs. I wanted my show to be over the top and impress the woman they called "Ms. B."

Chapter 24

The day of the show came in no time, but I felt prepared. I'd been shopping and compiled costumes for each number to be performed and I'd had my music prepared. I had my blinged out accessories that I liked to wear on stage to make me. I had developed my hairpieces and made sure I had what I needed cosmetics wise. I'd packed my bag the night before because I wanted to leave no room for error. I awoke the next morning to feel a familiar sensation. The unthinkable was happening. My throat was itchy and extremely sore. Fuck My Life! I wanted to impress "Ms. B" and here I was, unable to talk, much less, sing! I drank some green tea and lemon with hopes it would help my throat. I, also, used some Vick's vapor rub I kept handy for times like these. I scooped a nice glob with my index finger and sat it on the back of my tongue near my throat. I swallowed hard and nearly hurled it back up at the awful taste. I took another huge gulp of the tea. I tried to sing a note to test my remedy, but barely anything audibly came out. I was starting to panic. There was no way I was canceling and running the risk of Ms. B never again taking me seriously. I was going to try everything under the sun until those vocals were back full blast.

I showered, keeping my mouth open to let the steam hit my vocal cords, and dressed for work. Mondays were typically not a busy day at the salon, but for reasons, I can't explain we were packed. I was in no position to turn anyone down, so even with my anxiety building over my impending performance; I put my hairdresser hat on and serviced each client. It's a good thing that my talent with hair came naturally because my mind was everywhere but there. I was on autopilot and stressing hard about the night to come. I wanted to impress everyone, but primarily B. I can't lie I was taken by her immediately. She had a smoothness and fluidity about her and this gorgeous raspy voice. She was always neat and well dressed and exuded confidence. She had the most chiseled facial features and eyes that seemed to undress. I could tell upon our first encounter that she was intrigued by me as well by the way she looked at me and smiled. Not just any smile, but a "you just don't know!" kind of smile. When I started to sing, I sneaked a peek through my peripheral to see her smiling even harder. Yeah. I knew I had her, and she had me too.

That night I was performing at Burt's on Broadway. I got to the club before anyone else had. After being verified by the tall, husky man working as security, I asked him was there a holding area for the performers to dress. He directed me up a staircase to the upper of the bi-level club. I'd been at Burt's before but had never visited the second level. It was a beautiful entertainment space, with modern décor and plenty of room. The hardwood floors were waxed and exposed brick walls that housed floor to ceiling windows. There wasn't an actual stage, which I preferred, but there was a designated dance floor area that would serve as a makeshift one. The security officer led me to a room that was situated in the right-hand corner of the more substantial open space. He opened the door and motioned for me to go in. I thanked him and shut the door behind him as he turned to leave. I walked to the far end of the room where there were a long table and a few chairs. I put my bag down and looked into the full mirror fastened to the wall behind the table. I was a nervous wreck. Why was this happening? I'd done this very same thing countless times and for audiences large and small. Why was I stressing so hard over this one performance? My makeup was mainly done, but I opened my case to start putting on the finishing touches. I applied my false eyelashes and then some lipstick. I'd planned to rock the red fly hat I'd purchased earlier in the week with the hot red dress that fit like a glove for my first song, so I pinned my hair to the side, so the long curls cascaded down my right shoulder. I opened my jewelry case and selected opulent chandelier earrings and a matching cuff bracelet. Like any diva, I liked to shine on stage. I turned my attention to my rolling suitcase that held my attire for the evening. I unzipped it and pulled out that infamous red dress. This dress oozed sexuality, yet it had a certain elegance and grace. It hugged all the right places and demanded attention from all when I wore it. I pulled out the rhinestone encrusted strappy heels I had brought to compliment the dress and laid them both neatly on the table.

I examined my ensemble, and once I was satisfied, it was time for the moment of truth.

I pulled a small flask of cognac from my purse along with a vile of lemon juice. I squeezed a small amount of lemon into my mouth and then turned up the flask. The alcohol burned a little going down, but my nerves were so shot I hardly noticed. After stifling myself with the shot of liquor, I opened my mouth and attempted to sing. *"You Love Me."* I breathed a sigh of relief. My vocals were clear and back to normal. Much of my fear melted away at that moment. *"Especially Different..."* I continued. I loved to vocalize to Jill Scott. It was good cord exercise. I had time to kill before I hit the stage, so I decided to poke around a little and be nosey. I went back down to the lower level of the club and headed to the bar. I ordered a glass of white zinfandel from the gentleman standing behind it. Once I received my order, I took a seat at the far end. I scanned the room, and there was no sign of Ms. B or her crew. I was somewhat relieved, as my nerves hadn't completely dissipated. I sipped my drink and then decided to head back to my dressing room. I reached the dressing room and opened the door. There was another performer there by then, but I didn't recognize her, nor did I know what she'd come to do. "Hello," I said, extending my hand in an attempt to greet her. She didn't extend hers in return and only glanced up at my reflection in the mirror to return a simple, dry "Hi." I could take a hint, and I was no ass kisser, so I turned around and tended to my things. I gathered my belongings and pushed them to the far-left end of the long table, creating my space. If she wasn't going to be cordial, neither was I.

As I waited, I could hear the bustling sound of spectators starting to fill the space outside the door. This aroused my anxiety once again, yet I was excited to be getting closer to show time. I knew once I hit the stage and belted that initial note, I would be fine. Just then, there was a knock at the door. It startled me, but I reluctantly answered, "Come in…" The door slowly opened and there Ms. "B" in the flesh and looking damn good. I could smell her cologne from across the room, and it was as intoxicating as the drink I held in my hand.

Cracking a mischievous grin, she greeted me. "Hey, miss lady. How are you?" she began.

"I'm good, thank you. How are you?" I managed to reply.

"I'm doing well." She answered, now with a full-fledged smile. I smiled back nervously and adjusted my chair to face her. I could tell the other performer was ear hustling though she pretended not to be. I'd catch her out of the corner of my eye looking at both mine and B's reflection. B turned her attention to her and said flatly, "What's up? Angie?" Hey Bren, the fair-skinned woman replied. B turned her attention back to me and flashed that smile once again.

"I know I don't need to tell you this but break a leg!"

I giggled nervously and said "Thank you. I'll do my best."

"I'll see you out there," she said, as she pulled the door closed behind her. I breathed a sigh of relief. I was happy to see her, but my nerves were on a thousand as a result. What was it about this woman that aroused so much adrenaline in me? I didn't know, but at that point, I wanted to find out.

Just then there was another knock on the door. Before either the other girl or I could answer, in walked a man with a small crate in his hands. "Hello." he began. "I'm here to collect your music. What is your name and your number?' he asked me. I answered him and handed over my music. He repeated the process with the other performer and then left the room, closing the door behind him. I took to my little corner of the room and began to dress. I could hear the music pumping and the crowd circulating. I said a silent prayer as I dressed. Once my look was complete,

I took a seat in my little corner and waited. It wasn't long before I could hear the overture that would signal the beginning of the show. My stomach was in knots, but I tried to remain calm. The other performer was already dressed in what looked to me like regular street clothes, but when the M.C. announced the name "Angie B," she rose from her chair and left the room. I wasn't interested in watching or hearing her performance. Instead, I mentally played my songs in my mind. I had a slight buzz from the cognac and wine and was finally starting to feel like I was in my element.

I could hear faint applause, and then the M.C. announced, "Ladies and gentlemen, coming to the stage is Ms. Shae Mone!" I could hear clapping and cheering, and I took a deep breath and headed toward the dance floor. The D.J. held out the microphone for me as I passed by and the music began. I could feel a hint of nausea in the pit of my stomach as I took notice of every eye in the room piercing through me. I thought to myself, "Here it goes!"

"Baby, baby, baby... From the day I saw you. I wanted to catch your eye..." I relaxed a little as I started to sing and noticed people coming closer and paying more attention. As I'd recalled this mass reaction many times, I knew I had them. More importantly, I knew Ms. B was watching. Now I could officially show out. I continued to, and as I relaxed, my voice sounded smooth and sweet, like butter. I scanned the crowd, which was difficult due to the bright spotlight, and my eyes found her. I put on my most seductive walk and bedroom eyes and glided in her direction. I could see her eyes shifting nervously and her hands fidgeting. I got about three feet in front of her and began the second verse. "Oh! Baby, baby, baby, I see us on a first date doing' everything that makes me smile." The cutest grin cracked across her lips, and I thought "mission accomplished." Not wanting to be too conspicuous, I shifted and moved through the crowd, occasionally wooing a random woman or two with my melody. I finished the song, and the crowd erupted in applause. I concluded that my performance was well received based on the fact that the cheering continued through the M.C.'s attempt to calm the crowd and transition into the next performer's entrance. I said my thank you and blew kisses to the crowd and retreated to the dressing room.

Once there, I began to prepare for the next song. I pulled from my bag a floor-length, eggplant-colored sheer gown, with strategically placed appliqués. This dress was stunning and sensual but left little to the imagination. I chose it for this reason. I pulled out a matching eggplant thong and gold strappy stiletto sandals. I swapped dresses and stood in the mirror to examine myself. I was alone since the other performer had not returned to the dressing room. I was always a little self-conscious when I wore something as revealing as this. I was not skinny, but I was thick in the right places. I was too nervous to eat that day, so my stomach and waste were snatched, and the dress looked amazing on me. My breasts were surprisingly perky for their size and sat nicely behind the carefully placed beaded detailing. My ass cheeks were exposed, but somehow the dress looked tasteful. I adjusted my makeup to match the purple hues of my ensemble and applied my jewelry and shoes. I finished the last of my drink and cracked the door to listen for my cue. I heard the M.C. re-introduce me and I headed toward the makeshift stage. This time I could hear cheering and applause before I began to sing. I could see the stunned looks on some faces. I guess as a result of my "barely there" dress. I took a deep breath and began to do my thing once more. After I sang the second song, I thanked the audience and hurried to the dressing room to change. I exhaled once inside the privacy of the dressing room, relieved that my performance was over and went smoothly. I looked to my right and noticed that the performer called "Angie B" had gathered her belongings and appeared to have exited the dressing room for good. I was glad to have space to myself. I settled into a chair and started to disassemble. Just as I removed my earrings, there was a knock at the door.

I turned to answer, but before I could, it slowly creaked open. "Hey, Ms. Lady... You were on fire out there..." a familiar voice said. My eyes lit up and so did the butterflies in my stomach as Ms. B walked in and shut the door behind her.

"Thank you!" I exclaimed, cracking a huge smile, yet still trying to remain calm and cool. "That means a lot, coming from you..." I assured her, just slightly getting my flirt on. She flashed a nervous smile in return and blushed just a little.

"My partners and I are starting a weekly event here in this same venue, and we would love to have you as a regular on our show if you're interested..." she inquired.

"Sure. It would be a pleasure. "I answered without hesitation. Hell yeah. This was right up my alley. I would get to sing and be in the presence of Ms. "B," so how could I refuse?

She handed me an envelope with my name printed on it. "Thank you very much," I said.

"It was my pleasure. Thank you." She replied and held out her arms, signaling me for a hug. I stood to oblige, and she stepped back and hesitated. I was a little shocked and worried at the same time when I looked down and noticed that I was still scantily clad in that nakedly sheer dress. I laughed nervously, and so did she. Just as we were recovering from that awkward moment, she embraced me, and I damn near fainted. She smelled so damn good, almost intoxicating. The warmth of her touch on the small of my back melted me instantly. She held on for what seemed like forever and just as I was sure my thong would start to become wet, we were jarred from our connection as the door abruptly flung open. Seeming just as stunned as we were, Angie B had returned to retrieve the package of Newport cigarettes she'd left behind. As we parted ways and tried to regain our composure without looking suspicious, she looked at me curiously, then at Ms. B. She shuffled past us and scooped up the cigarettes at the right end of the long table. She turned to walk in the direction of the exit, but not before looking at Ms. "B" once more and giving a long, disapproving roll of her eyes. She left the room, shutting the door behind her.

I couldn't exactly figure out what it was about her that turned me on however it became more intense when she said, "Well I hope you're going to stick around and enjoy the rest of the night."

"I think I will for a minute," I said, still trying to play it cool.

"Good." She said, cracking that familiar grin. She turned and exited the room. I exhaled and smiled hard thinking about our embrace. I never believed in love at first sight, but this woman had me feeling some way. We hadn't been on a date or even had a phone conversation, but she was heavily on my mind and even more so now that I'd had physical contact with her. All I could think about was the next time I would have the chance to interact with her. I hurried and undressed and slipped into a sexy, Ruched black dress and matching strappy stilettos. I let my hair hang down and slid on a seductive red lip. I gathered my things and stowed them in a corner altogether, not wanting to lug the rolling suitcase through the crowded club. I grabbed the purse from the table and headed out of the dressing room and into the crowd.

Chapter 25

I entered the area the party was taking place, I could hear Jackie O blasting through the sound system. *"Pussy Real Good... That Pussy Real Good..."* The lyrics said. As raunchy as that song was, I liked it. It had a banging beat, and you almost couldn't help but bop your head to it. I turned my attention to the makeshift stage and saw a heavyset, light-skinned woman, in a too-tight black latex dress, lip-syncing to the song. She was cute in the face and had long wavy micro braids in her hair. Though the dress didn't compliment her, she was cute, and the crowd seemed to receive her. They were singing along to the song and tipping her as she performed it. I watched as she finished her set. The audience applauded as she left the stage and went over to a table to sit down. I guess she'd come already dressed to perform, as I hadn't seen her in the common dressing room.

My eyes searched the room for Ms. "B," but I didn't find her. Just then, I spotted Corrine walking toward me.

"Sup beautiful?" she greeted me as she held out her hands and motioned for a hug.

"Hey, Corrine. Where's Rae?" I inquired as I hugged her. She shrugged as if to say she had no idea. I didn't want to pry, as sometimes their relationship was a sensitive subject. As awkward as things had been since the encounter between the three of us, I just wanted things to go back to normal and for them to be happy together. Rae was such a dear friend to me, and I knew how deeply in love she was with Corrine, but aside from me, Corrine just had other ideas. She was frivolous when it came to other women and apparently wanted to sew her oats. She took care of home and was a great provider to Rae, but that was just an exchange for being able to play the field. I think Rae's whole objective with incorporating me into their sex life was an attempt at keeping Corrine at home, but Corrine, ultimately, had other agendas.

"I'm going to the bar. Do you want anything?" She inquired.

"Sure. I want a White Zinfandel, thank you." I requested.

"I got you." She assured me, winking her right eye. Corrine was smooth, funny and mad fine, so it was no surprise that straight women flocked to her. She was very masculine in her mannerisms and demeanor, yet her physical features were soft and feminine. She had a flawless buttery complexion and naturally curly black hair that she wore cropped in a short Caesar haircut. She had gorgeous eyes that hid behind the cutest, slightly tinted wire-framed glasses. She was about five feet eight with athletic build and abs you could do laundry on. She was a great dancer and just fun to be around in general. She and Rae made the most adorable couple, and though she initiated it, I didn't feel right being this third party in their relationship. I loved them both dearly and just wanted to see them happy together. I was never the third wheel, and I wanted a woman of my own as well.

I shifted my attention and began to survey the room again, looking for my crush. Instead, my eyes landed on the woman who had performed last. I had a strange feeling that someone was watching me and sure enough, the woman seated next to her with her hand cupped over her mouth, whispering in her ear, was none other than Angie B, the performer I'd shared a dressing room with earlier. It didn't take a genius to figure out that I was their topic, judging by how they were now both staring at me. I tried to pay them no mind and continued to look for "B." I hadn't seen her since our encounter earlier that night and was beginning to wonder where she could be. Corrine returned and handed me the drink she'd gotten for me. We sipped and made small talk as the event came to a close. She offered to accompany me to the dressing room to retrieve my things. We went into the dressing room and started to gather my belongings when suddenly the music stopped, and we could hear a loud argument and commotion in the space outside. Corrine grabbed the rolling suitcase as I scooped up my belongings and we headed for the door. Before we could make our way toward the staircase, a fight had broken out. There was a large mob around what appeared to be two women, a femme, and a stud, in a physical altercation. I tried to understand what was going on when Corrine put her hand up to block me from walking forward. "Stay back." She commanded, and I listened. I stood behind her out of the way of the large crowd and tried to process the scene. Hands were swinging wildly as the club's security attempted to control the situation. As the burly bouncers pulled the two women apart and loudly instructed the crowd that had gathered around them to fall back, I could see the identity of the two women who had been fighting. It was the woman who had performed the Jackie O song. Before I could inquire Corrine escorted me out of the club, and we headed home.

I couldn't wait to ask her what that whole commotion with "B" and the woman in the black dress was about, but before I could, she blurted out, "So that was Mesha, Brenda's woman." "The one she was fighting with?" I inquired.

"Yeah," Corrine confirmed.

"Wow..." I said, putting it all together. I was still oblivious, being that I didn't see exactly how the fight started, but now it all made sense. Maybe when I'd noticed the two of them staring at me, Angie B had been telling Mesha how she'd walked in on Ms. B, and I was embracing in the dressing room, and Mesha had decided to confront her. On the ride home, Corrine filled me in on Mesha and B's relationship. She told me how Mesha was a parasite and how she and her six illegitimate children were living off of B. How their relationship was on the rocks because Mesha was rumored to be having outside affairs with men, which she preferred. From what I understood, B was just a convenient financial host. Corrine, also, told me how B would confide in her and how unhappy she was. B had a young son of her own, but Mesha and her children had taken over. They terrorized and destroyed the home that she'd inherited after her mother's untimely passing, and Mesha rarely chastised them or tried to bring resolution to the situation. She spent B's money, drove her cars and disrespected her in every way possible. This made me extremely sad. I already liked B and couldn't help but wonder how someone could be so cruel, especially to someone like her. She had a sweet, shyness about her that made me want to be there for her. I've never been one to step on the next woman's toes or try to wreck a happy home, but I felt like B deserved so much more and I was going to be just the one to give it to her, and I'd decided then that Mesha's time was up.

Chapter 26

I had only been home for a few moments before the ringing of my cell phone startled me. It was nearly three o'clock a.m. so I couldn't imagine who might be calling. Corrine opened the apartment door, and I followed her inside and headed for my room. I sat my bags down and scrambled through my purse for my phone. Just as I fished it from the large black handbag, it stopped ringing. I sighed, disappointed that I hadn't caught it, but maybe whoever it was would leave a message. I pressed the menu button to check the missed call log, but I didn't recognize the number.

I nearly jumped when it suddenly started to ring again. "Hello?" I inquired.

"Hey... It's B..." she began. I'd wanted to call and check for her to make sure she was ok after the fiasco at the club but didn't want to pry. I figured maybe she needed some space. But I was relieved when she reached out to me.

"Are you alright?" I asked. "I was worried about you, but I didn't want to bombard you with phone calls and questions."

"I'm fine physically, but mentally, I don't know." She answered. "In four years, Mesha and I have never had a physical altercation. I'm not sure I can go on with her like this." She finished.

"I feel partly responsible. I didn't know that she and Angie were friends and maybe she took seeing us hug the wrong way." I said, trying to take some of the pressure off of her.

"I'm sure she ran back and told her some embellished version of what she saw. I was chilling with my boys one minute, and the next Mesha had her fingers in my face, calling me every name under the sun. I got so much going on right now. This drama is the last thing I need." She said.

"I know, and I'm so sorry that you're going through all of this." I offered. "Where are you now? Is she with you? Are you safe?" I asked.

"She's at the house, and I haven't gone back there. It's a shame that I don't feel comfortable going to my own house. I know she's still heated and wants to fight and I just can't deal with it right now. I'm just riding." She stated.

"Come pick me up. I want to ride with you." I declared, surprised by my boldness.

She agreed and, within minutes, was out in front of the building. I made my outside to her car. She pressed the power lock to let me into the passenger door. I felt butterflies hit me as I slipped into the seat next to her. "Hey..." she said, smiling and blushing at the same time. She never really looked me in the eyes, and I couldn't tell if it was shyness or embarrassment that was the cause. I could see red scratches on her neck and face where Mesha had clawed at her. I took her face into my hands and looked into her eyes. In her eyes were so much pain and sadness. When they say, "the eyes are the windows to the soul," whoever it was - was dead ass on.

"It's ok baby. I'm here for you. You don't have to be ashamed." I assured her. A tear rolled down her face and onto my thumb. I hugged her and held her tight. She wrapped her arms around my waist and hugged me tighter. She pulled back to release me and then grabbed my face and kissed me. I kissed her back, and we tongued passionately, never coming undone from our embrace. At that moment, I knew I had fallen. I was in a love-struck trance, and I wanted to know everything that had to do with Brenda Wyatt, A.K.A. Ms. "B." She threw the car in drive, and we headed toward Telegraph Rd. We were each exhausted but way too high off of our connection to want to separate. We were approaching a motel, and I suggested that we stop and get a room. We pulled into the parking lot and checked in. We went into the motel room, and she took off the heavy coat she'd been wearing. I hung my jacket in the closet and sat on the corner of the bed. I studied her. She seemed to be going through so much mentally. I wanted to encourage her to open up, but I didn't want to pry. I wanted to learn everything about her, but I knew that there was a time and place. I wanted her to feel comfortable with me and for things to flow naturally. I wanted her to trust me. I turned to her as she took a seat in a chair next to the bed. I took her hand in mine and held it firmly.

"I'm a great listener if you want to talk" I began. There was a moment of awkward silence, and I could tell she was still not ready to be transparent. The events of that night had penetrated her deeply, and it was painfully apparent. Her eyes welled up again. "What is it, baby? You can talk to me..." I coached, trying to comfort her. I leaned in closer to her and grabbed her other hand.

"I just don't know how to let her go. She's been my life for nearly the last four years. I know things are crazy, but we have a family. I have a son that she helped raise." She explained. "She has kids that I love as my own, and I can't imagine not being in their lives. I don't know what to do. But I'm so fucking unhappy." She ended her sentence which gave the tears permission to fall.

I cradled her in my arms. It was such an awkward moment, I was sincerely concerned about where I stood with her, given the fact that we had just kissed, and I knew my feelings for her were already significant and growing. I could understand the push and pull associated with the breakup of a long-term relationship. Aside from the trauma and embarrassment of the events that had taken place that night, I could tell that she was reeling emotionally and now was not the time to discuss the particulars of the direction in which she and I would go. All she needed right now was comfort and peace, something that she lacked at home. I turned down the bed and fluffed the pillows. I went over to her and knelt down to remove her shoes. She stood and lifted the heavy sweater she'd been wearing and exposed the t-shirt she wore underneath. She unfastened her jeans and stepped out of them. I took her hand and led her to the bed. She sat on the edge and looked at me. I turned and reached around to unzip my dress. I could feel her eyes on me as my dress fell to the floor, exposing the black, lacey thong and bra I wore underneath. I crawled into bed from the opposite side as her eyes followed me. I reached for her arm to pull her toward me. She wrapped her arms around me and held me. I reached up and caressed her cheek, and she leaned in to kiss me. We kissed and held each other and were soon fast asleep.

Chapter 27

We were still holding each other as the sun rose. The alarm on B's phone had sounded, but I was already awake. I couldn't help but think about the events of the night prior and just what would be our next step. I was pretty sure I was falling for B, but she, technically, still had a woman and I had a feeling Mesha would be very reluctant to let go so smoothly. From what I understood, her reasons for holding on to B had nothing to do with love, but purely the stability that she had provided her. I knew that she knew something was up with B and me, and the next time she and I met, she'd try and come for me. Though I didn't particularly care for drama or confrontation, I was fully prepared to flip out if it found me. Contrary to what some believed, I didn't like to argue or fight. Exchanging unkind words or physical blows with anyone left me feeling empty. I just happened to be predisposed to such because growing up, that's all I knew. I learned at an early age to solve a conflict with curse words and my fists. This unspoken anger fueled me for as long as I could remember, but it was impossible for me to pin down the point at which it stemmed. I just knew that at even the thought of a perceived threat, I could go from zero to a hundred and like, quick.

I could feel B stirring beneath me as she pawed at the nightstand, fumbling for her cell phone. "What time is it, baby?" she inquired, her hand still searching. I craned my neck toward my side of the bed where the alarm clock was.

"Five -fifty- eight, sweetheart," I answered.

"Aw Shit!" she exclaimed, in almost a whisper.

"What? What's wrong?" I asked.

"I need to get to the store." She said hastily, nearly hopping back into her jeans. She was the manager of one of the most popular car detailing stores in the city. It was part of a massive franchise, and there was one on every corner. As a manager, she made excellent money, but there was also a lot of responsibility. She oversaw all of the operations of that store. She did the hiring and firing and handled customer concerns, as well as, managed the money that the store took in. That, coupled with the stress she was experiencing at home, I could imagine would weigh on anybody. She finished dressing and finally located her cell phone. Her face fell as she saw that she had over thirty missed calls from Mesha.

"I know when I finally do go home; it's going to be some shit." She sighed, shaking her head. She punched the keys on the phone and put it to her ear. "Ayo Rinne. You made it to the store yet?" she inquired. "Martin's not there, is he? Ok. Good. Go ahead and set up. I'm five minutes away." She hung up and stepped into her shoes. She hurried over to me and kissed my forehead. "Stay here. I'm coming back and get you in a few." She assured me.

"Ok baby." I agreed and returned a kiss to her lips. She scooped up her coat and headed out of the door. I lay back on the bed, thinking. How would this play out? Though I didn't know a lot about B, I knew how I felt. Even with my first love in high school, feelings only developed over time. But this was different. I was drawn to her. She and I just had a few interactions, and yet I couldn't stop thinking about her. The way she looked; smelled, and her sexy raspy voice when she talked. She had swag and innocence about her. She hadn't yet opened up to me about her personal life or past, but the sadness in her eyes made me want to learn everything there was to know and how to comfort her. I wondered how her son and I would get along being that Mesha had been the only other parent he'd known. I asked how their impending split would affect him as well as the other children. Though I didn't have children of my own, being the eldest of all of my siblings gave me a maternal edge. I just hoped that everything would work out smoothly because I was sure that I wanted to become a fixture in B's world.

I drifted back off to sleep, still drowsy from the night before. My nightmares had become even more frequent since I'd been attacked and slept next to B had been the first time in months I'd felt safe and not afraid or unable to get to sleep. I must've dozed pretty heavily because this one was especially horrific and graphics. In the dream, I was being raped, but the man committing the unspeakable act had no facial features, just a blank canvas of dark skin beneath a short afro of hair. I was crying and begging him to stop, but my pleas seemed to fall on deaf ears as he kept violently pounding. He was heavy on top of me, and his breathing was deep and labored. I was young in the dream, maybe nine or ten and he was at least thirty. He had my arms pressed against the cold, hard surface we were on, and his sweat dripped down onto my face, making me cry even harder. He stunk, kind of like cigarettes and funk, sort of the way my father's room always smelled. It was still a pigsty in there. Old food and dishes stacked on top of furniture. Candy wrappers littering the floor while the ever-present stench of soiled laundry and cigarettes would knock you back each time you opened the door. I jumped when I was jarred from that horror by the sound of the motel room door opening. I quickly sat up in the bed, relieved to see that it was B. "Hey baby! Are you asleep?" she inquired. I hurriedly patted my hair down and tried to collect myself, still wanting to look pretty for her. I rubbed my eyes and looked over at the clock on the nightstand. It was now ten forty-two, nearly time for checkout. I knew B probably had to be back at work, so I threw my dress and shoes on from the night before and gathered my phone and purse.

Chapter 28

We got into her sleek, silver Mitsubishi and headed down Eight Mile Road, towards my complex. There was an awkward silence between us as during the ride, and I couldn't help but wonder what was on her mind. Before I could ask, she said "I'm not going home tonight either, and I don't want to be alone. Will you stay with me?" I tracked what I'm sure was a broad smile as I happily agreed. "I'll call you when I get off." She promised as we pulled up to my building. She kissed me, and I exited the car and headed inside. I went straight to my room, not bothering to check to see if my roommates were home. I set my purse down and kicked off my shoes. I flopped down on the bed, deep in thought. I wondered if B was feeling me as much as I was feeling her. Up until now, I had played it cool, not wanting to come off as easy or hard up, but things were rapidly starting to shift. I didn't like the idea of her going back to that house and sleeping next to another woman. I wanted to be the one she slept next to every night. The idea that things could suddenly go in reverse scared me, and I found myself in fear of the thought of her not being in my life. I wanted to be her woman, not

Mesha. I tried not to over think things. I took off my clothes and headed for the shower.

Over the next two weeks, B and I continued to see each other. We went on dates and talked on the phone every day. I was fascinated with her, and the feeling seemed to be mutual. My best friend from high school was getting married, and I was her maid of honor. I asked B to accompany me to the wedding, and she happily agreed. My best friend, Erin, wasn't having a bachelorette party, so we decided we would go out and bar hop instead. We'd gone to a couple of local spots, but the night just didn't seem to be taking off the way your last night as a single woman should, so I made a suggestion. Though Erin wasn't gay, she'd never been judgmental toward me. She'd been supportive and had even hung out with my ex and me at a few of the gay clubs. Club Palladium was popping on Friday nights, and I knew we would have a good, drunken time there. It was always packed, and the entertainment and drinks were on point. It was the hottest gay club in Detroit, so I suggested we go. We got there and, as usual, the line was wrapped around the building. A favorite exotic dancer was scheduled to perform so what was standing room only on a regular was even more insane tonight. Every lesbian in the "D" had come to see Ms. OOZIE. After standing in line forever, we finally paid and got in. I wasted no time getting my friend liquored up and making sure she was having a good time. Erin was shy and introverted. She was three days younger than me, but our personalities couldn't be more opposite. She was reserved, and I was the boisterous, outspoken wild child. I wanted her to let her hair down and have a great time tonight.

We drank like a fish and bopped our heads to the loud house music. Erin wasn't a drinker, so halfway through her second cocktail; she had definitely loosened up. The DJ announced that Ms. Oozie was coming to the stage and about 90% of the people in the club made a beeline to crowd around it. I'd seen Ms. Oozie perform once before and she was terrific to watch. She was a great exotic dancer, and though she was only about five feet tall and 120 pounds, she was extremely flexible and robust. She could do all kinds of contortionist tricks, and she would pick people from the audience who were twice her size and toss them around like rag dolls as part of the show. Though she was an exotic dancer, her act wasn't raunchy or all about acts of sex. It was an artistic mix of dancing, body mechanics, and crowd participation. We drank, laughed, partied and watched in awe as Ms. Oozie picked one burly lesbian after another from the audience and bench pressed them with her feet. I could tell that my friend was enjoying herself and that made me happy. As two a.m. rolled around, we decided to call it a night. I'd decided to stay the night at Erin's to help her prepare for the wedding. Her 15-month-old daughter had stayed with her mom while we'd gone out and her fiancé was in the navy and stationed in Illinois so that it would be just the two of us there. I'd met her fiancé only a handful of times due to him being absent and in the military. He seemed ok to me, and as long as my friend was happy, I was delighted for her. We were pulling into Erin's driveway when I got a call from B.

"Hello?" I inquired, delighted to hear from her.

"Hey, baby. Where you at? I'm about to pull up on you. I need to see you." She demanded.

"I'm on the eastside at Erin's. I'm staying the night." I answered, smiling from ear to ear.

"What's her address? I'm coming' through." She declared. After asking Erin if it was ok, I told her the address, and she let me know that she was on her way. I secretly liked that bossy way she said to me that she was coming rather than asking. It was like she needed to see me, and nothing were going to get in her way. I was mad turned on and couldn't wait to see her. Somehow, I knew tonight would be the night that things would officially turn serious with her and me.

Erin, having had more alcohol than she was used to, retired to her room as soon as we got in. I showered and waited for B to arrive. When she did, I let her in, and we went into the guestroom. Before I could even correctly greet her, she kissed me with more passion than ever. This revved my engine even more, and I was instantly wet. I tore at her jacket, and she kissed and rubbed me even more. She pushed me down onto the sofa and snatched off my pajama pants. She spread my legs and wasted no time putting her lips on mine. She felt better than I had imagined. I tried to contain my excitement, but before long I was singing her name.

I'd received good head before, but this was on a whole other level. My legs were shaking, and my heart was pounding fast. I exploded in her mouth at least three times in quick succession, but she kept right on eating. It was as if my orgasms fueled her. The louder I moaned, and the more I shook, the more intense she became. Finally, as I was sure I was going to pass out, she stopped and came up. I was panting as if I'd run a marathon and I saw her crack a naughty grin. Maybe she got a kick out of sucking my soul from me. Either way, I was in deep shit. She leaned in and kissed me softly, her chin and lips still wet from my multiple orgasms. I couldn't talk and be still trying to compose myself when she went back down. Just when I thought I couldn't produce any more juices, I did three more times. I was mentally fucked up. I'd already had feelings for her, but this magnified things by a thousand. She got up and asked where the bathroom was. Still unable to speak, I pointed across the hall. She went and, I assume, washed her face and returned. I was lying on the sofa in disbelief when she came and lay on top of me. She kissed me and caressed my face. The dim lighting from the TV allowed me to see her face. We locked eyes for a second and said, "I love you."

It was euphoric and wasted no time saying, "I love you too, baby." The truth was, I more than loved her. I was madly in love with her. I'd felt it for a while now but was afraid to say it. B was hard to read so I wasn't sure if she felt the same way. I was relieved to know that the feeling was reciprocated. She snuggled in closer to me, and we drifted off to sleep.

We were only asleep for a couple of hours when she awakened me with a kiss. She'd already gotten up and dressed and was kneeling over me.

"I got to go, sweetheart." She told me.

"Now?", I inquired in a sleepy voice. "Yeah but I'll see you later at the wedding." She assured me. She reached into her coat pocket and pulled something out. She opened my hand and put in it a cell phone.

"I want to be able to reach you at all times." She declared. I was pleasantly surprised.

"Ok baby." I obeyed. She reached for my hand and pulled me up from the sofa. She wrapped her arms around me and kissed me passionately. With every touch or kiss from her, my love for her was growing. I could feel it all through me. I had loved before, but this was different. I was entranced.

I walked her to the door, and we kissed again. This time, I was the first to say "I love you" before watching her walk to her car. I just stood at the door in awe and not sure what to make of what I was feeling. I wanted this woman so bad. I wanted to be with her every second of every day. I wanted to be the one to wash away all of the pain of her past. I knew we'd only been dating a few weeks, but I could barely recall my life before her. My mind was officially blown. I was briefly snapped back to reality when Erin approached from behind and said, in a raspy, labored voice, "Good morning." I turned to see her in the kitchen, fumbling with the coffee pot.

"Well good morning sleeping' beauty." I chuckled, amused at her disheveled appearance. At first glance, she appeared to have come out of a coma, the way her hair piled together at the top of her head, and she had on panties, a camisole, one blue sock, and one green sock.

"Bitch if I don't make it to the altar, I'm going to kill you." She warned. I erupted in laughter.

"I got you boo! I would off myself before I let you miss your wedding. You'll be a little hung over, that's all." I joked. She chugged the pink mug of coffee she'd poured and tried to pull herself together. We each showered and ran through our checklist to be sure we didn't forget anything. We loaded the dresses and other Items into the car and headed for the chapel. J.D., Erin's fiancé, called to say that he'd arrived in Detroit and would see us soon. That visibly put her at ease. The anxiety had registered all over Erin's face that morning. I tried to do whatever I could to minimize her stress.

Chapter 29

We were the first to arrive at the chapel, and a short, caramel skinned, the grey-haired woman let us in. She directed us back to a dressing room at the rear of the building. The chapel had been pre-decorated, which took one thing off of my list of things to do. I hung the dresses and laid out the shoes and accessories. Erin sat down at the small vanity in the corner of the room. I plugged in the curling iron and started on her makeup while the curlers heated up. She dialed her mother repeatedly, who hadn't gotten to the chapel, but to no avail. I could see the panic on her face and tried to distract her.

"What kind of eyeshadow do you want a smoky eye or lavender shadow?" I asked.

"Smoky." She hastily said, obviously blowing me off. "Would you like a bold lip or nude lip?" I attempted again.

"Bold! Nude! I don't care!" she exclaimed, this time the irritation apparent in her response. I knew then to shut up.

"Where the hell are you? I've been calling' you for thirty minutes!" She demanded into the receiver.

"I'm coming girl!" I could hear her mother screaming at the other end. "Hello? Hello!" Erin inquired to an obviously dead opposite end. "Her stupid ass hung up on me! She was supposed to have been here with the bouquets!" Erin cried in frustration.

"Calm down, E. She'll be here. It's all going to work out." I tried to console her. She all but ignored me while she, then, tried to get her fiancé on the phone.

"JD, where are you?" she demanded. "No! I need you to get here now!" she warned.

"Turn around and see how pretty you look." I tried again to deflect her attention. She did as I instructed and burst into tears.

I was just about to panic when she said, "Oh my God. I look beautiful!" I breathed a sigh of relief and laughed a little to myself. Erin had always been a crybaby. She even got emotional when I sang happy birthday to her when we were in high school. I was just happy that she was happy with her look on her special day. I situated her veil behind her upswept hair and securely pinned it in place. Just then, her sister, August, walked in. August was Erin's sister by her father. She'd asked her to be a bridesmaid in the wedding, but they weren't all that close. They greeted each other and hugged, and August and I proceeded to help Erin get into the difficult, corseted dress. Once we securely laced her up in the gown,

152

we each got into our dresses. Just as we did, Erin's mother, Mrs. Small walked in. She had a bag in hand with burgundy and white bouquets in it. Erin rolled her eyes and exhaled at the same time. Just then, she received a text message. I looked at the buzzing cell phone and running across the top of the screen were the words "I'm here." from JD. "JD is here, E," I informed her. Her face brightened up. August knelt down and fastened her shoes for her. "OKAY! Let's do this!" she exclaimed. We each took our bouquets from the bag her mother had bought and waited for the organist's cue.

When it was my turn to march down the aisle, I scanned the room until I found my love. She was proudly sitting on a pew behind Erin's family, looking so handsome. She wore tan slacks and a tan Coogi sweater. Her hair in a low-cut Caesar with understated gold jewelry. I could've ripped her clothes off right then. I got to the altar, and the minister handed me the microphone.

I began to sing as Erin came down the aisle. "I believe in you and me..." JD smiled from ear to ear as she walked toward him. You could hear their 1-year old daughter cooing and cheering them on as they said their "I Do's." My friend appeared to be happy, and I was truly happy for her. I didn't know JD well, but he seemed to be nice, and I was just ecstatic to see my friend enjoying life. After the wedding, we went back to Erin's mother's house for dinner. B had accompanied me, and we stayed a while and laughed and talked with the newlyweds and family.

As the evening drew to a close, B and I said our goodbyes and made our way to her car. She was still technically living with Mesha, but I knew I didn't want to be without her tonight. I told her I wanted to get a room and we headed toward our little spot on Telegraph. Once inside the room, I headed toward the bathroom with the overnight bag I had brought with me. I stepped into the shower and turned it on. I stood under it and began to lather up. I heard the door open and shut and then the screeching of the shower curtain hooks against the rail as it was being pulled open. Then I felt her hands on me. She rubbed and caressed my body and kissed the back of my neck. Chills ran through me as she made her way down, kissing my spine. She grabbed my waist and spun me around to face her. She knelt down and lifted my left leg, resting my foot on the edge of the tub. Without hesitation, she furiously licked and sucked my womanhood, leaving no part untouched. Before long I was singing her name. She let me erupt a couple of times before taking my hand and leading me to the king-sized bed. She laid me down and walked over to the chair where she'd sat her bag down. This was the first time I had seen her naked. I was shocked. Up until now, she'd always dressed in loose-fitting, men's clothes so it was somewhat impossible to tell how her body was shaped. Her frame was small, and though she's a woman, somehow, I'd imagined her straight up and down with a sort of masculine build. I was way off. This woman had the body of a goddess. I'd been a dancer for close to six years and had never seen a body as perfect and chiseled as hers. She had a tiny waist, about 24 inches, and hips and ass for days! I was in awe and found myself even more turned on. I just watched in silence as she stood there, rummaging through the black duffel bag. She finally fished out a strap harness, with an eight-inch dildo. She situated it around her legs and waist and walked back over to the bed. I was excited, nervous and turned on all at once. She started kissing me again and positioned herself between my legs. She pushed forward into me, and I gasped. She began thrusting slowly and kissing my neck and ears. She felt unbelievably good, and my sounds let her know it. She picked up her pace a little, and I sang even louder. "Yes, Baby! Don't stop!" I pleaded. She pounded harder, and I exploded, but she didn't stop. Now she was kissing me furiously and fucking the shit out of me. I was screaming her name and came so many times I lost count. She was like a machine, and I was lost in ecstasy. She finally slowed to a stop and kissed me softly. I couldn't speak and was still panting from having my vagina detached from me. I could feel that the sheets under me were wet. She lay on top of me and rested her head on my breasts. I hadn't been the one doing the work, but I was exhausted. The next thing I remember was the daylight shining faintly through the sheer drapes of the motel room window.

Chapter 30

Over the next few days, B and I spent all of our spare time virtually together. I wasn't at all concerned that we were moving too fast, even though it had only been a couple of weeks. I was emotionally invested, and that made it worth it to me. We'd gone on dates, and she even introduced me to her three-year-old son, Angelo. He was a shy, introverted child. I tried to interact with him, but I could tell he wasn't much for strangers. I didn't have any children of my own, but I'd helped raise all of my siblings, being that I was the eldest, and I wanted to establish a relationship with him if his mother and I were going to be together. His fourth birthday was in a few days, and there was to be a bowling party, something she and him enjoyed doing together. I was aware that Mesha and her kids would be there, so I was prepared to sit this one out. It was still unclear, however, whether or not Mesha new the extent of mine and B's interaction and what exactly was to come of their situation. I would never dream of asking B to throw a woman and her children onto the street, but I was becoming anxious because I wanted her to myself. Sure, she was spending most of her time with me and assured me that they hadn't been sexually active for months, but that wasn't enough at this point. I wanted to know what was next. The holidays were approaching, and all I wanted for Christmas was Ms. B.

The night that Angelo's party was scheduled, I got a phone call from B. "Hey baby. What's up?" I inquired.

"Hey." She responded flatly. I could immediately tell something was wrong by how she sounded.

"Why you sound like that, baby? What's wrong? Did the party turn out alright?" I questioned.

"Yeah, Listen... I can't see you anymore. I'm sorry." She said and abruptly hung up the phone. I was floored. In about 30 seconds I went from shocked to confuse and right into being furious. I angrily punched the keys on my cell phone and dialed her back. When she answered, I didn't even give her the chance to speak.

"What the fuck do you mean you can't see me anymore, B?" I demanded.

"Mesha and I are working it out and I just can't. You wouldn't understand. We got history. My son loves her. I just can't break up our family. I'm sorry." She explained. This time I hung up and burst into tears. It felt like my heart broke. I was devastated. I felt used and thrown away. What was worse is I didn't see it coming. I was sure, judging by our recent progression, that we were on the same page and an upward incline. I was horrified to know that I'd been wrong. I peeled myself up from the tearful heap I'd become on the sofa and walked to the kitchen to grab the tequila. Shot after shot, I poured trying, to no avail, to make myself numb. This pain was too much. I wanted to call and curse her out, but at the same time, I tried to beg her to reconsider. I was madly in love with her, and I couldn't believe she'd pass up someone who would love and want her and fulfill her every desire to be with someone who was sucking dick on the side and abusing her kindness. Before long, I was drunk and angry, and I wanted an explanation. I threw on my coat and boots and went for the keys to Rae's truck. I pulled up in front of B's house and flipped open my cell phone. I called her and demanded that she come outside and face me. She did, but she wasn't alone. Mesha had followed her and was walking toward the truck. I unfastened my seatbelt and reached for the lever to open the driver side door.

"Do not get out of the car!" B demanded as she turned to face Mesha who was now on her heels. I watched as she tried unsuccessfully to calm her. She was holding her by both forearms, but Mesha continued to rant.

"You brought your ass to my house! She barked!"

"Yeah, and I got your bitch!" I retorted, reaching for the lever again. Before I could exit the truck, B had run around to the driver side and stopped me.

"Please! Let me handle this! It was NOT a good idea to show up here!" she reprimanded. "Stay the fuck on the sidewalk, Mesha! Let me handle this!" She instructed. Mesha listened but was still talking mad shit from her position on the sidewalk. I was too upset, to even hear what she was saying. I started crying again. "Please understand" she began. "I have to think about what's good for my son. Our timing is just bad right now. Please..." she nudged. Though hurt and confused, my pride and the anger I was feeling wouldn't let me continue to make a fool of myself. This was her position, and I had to accept it. Without saying another word, I pulled off. I got to the corner and erupted in tears.

The succession of tears continued for days. Not only did I feel rejected, but I felt thrown away and once again, not good enough. It hadn't been drilled into my head previously that I was ugly, but this made me feel ugly and defective. What did Mesha have that I didn't? Six bad assed, illegitimate children were all I could come up with. I sulked for days, questioning my worth. Why had everyone that I held so dear view me as expendable? Was I just that basic and replaceable? Even my parents hadn't valued me and put me on that pedestal as I'd seen so many parents do with their children. They had used me to express whatever sadistic emotion had been plaguing them at the time so; surely, this must be what I deserved.

After days of moping and crying, I'd decided that I needed some air. I'd gotten the attention of one of the hottest new party promoters on the L.G.B.T. scene, and he'd asked me to perform on his weekly night at Club Innuendo. L.J. was quickly gaining notoriety as the "Guy for the Girls." At that time, the Gay entertainment world was largely focused on female impersonation performers. There were hardly any bio women performing, and an all-female review was almost unheard of. L.J.

revolutionized the bio-girl performance platform on the Detroit gay scene. I always wanted girls like me to have a place and an audience under the LGBT umbrella to showcase our talents as well, so I jumped at the chance when asked to be one of the first acts. Club Innuendo had been an immediate hit since it had gone under new ownership and went from an inactive strip club to a gay club. It began to bang once it became known as an avenue for the girls. Tonight, was no different and it was standing room only. I was happy to be out and not hiding in the confines of my looming depression. I'd been drinking already and was ready to perform and have a good time. After bypassing the "airport security," I headed straight for the bar and ordered Hennessy and cranberry juice. After getting my order, I made a beeline for the dressing room. I took a seat at the L shaped counter and began to put the finishing touches on my makeup. I was slightly buzzing and that coupled with the music lifted my spirits a little, if only temporarily. I was in the middle of perfecting my smoky eye when I caught the reflection of the dressing room door opening behind me in the huge mirror that lined the counter where I was seated. I damn near fell out of the chair when I saw who was coming in. It was B. I tried hard to keep my composure, but I was stunned. Only seconds had passed before I could feel a rush of emotions creeping up on me. I wanted to cry, scream, run and hug her all at the same time. Still, I had to hold it together. I looked down at my eyeshadow palette to avoid making eye contact with her, but I felt her eyes trained on me. I felt her walking up close to me, but I didn't look up.

"Can I talk to you?" she inquired, resting her hand on my shoulder. I felt hot tears well up in my eyes, but I fought them back, refusing to show her my vulnerability.

"There is nothing for us to talk about. "I managed to say. Then I closed my makeup case, got up and walked out of the dressing room. I barely made it to the stall in the ladies' room before the tears fell. Why was I so emotional? After all, I had only known this woman for roughly a month so why was her mere presence enough to invoke such intense feelings? I had to pull it together. I not only had a show to do but the fact that I now knew she would be watching upped the pressure that much more. I couldn't let her know how she was affecting me. I wiped my face, composed myself and exited the ladies room. I returned to the dressing room just as the overture was being played. Much to my relief, B was gone. I took my same seat at the counter and tried to remain calm. The show went in order of the documented lineup, and I nervously awaited my turn. I heard the M.C. announce my name and I put on my confidence and headed for the stage. I performed well, considering my heart was doing somersaults. I almost never rushed through a performance, but I just wanted to get it over with.

I stepped down from the eminent stage and walked briskly to the dressing room. I avoided scanning the crowd but secretly wondered if B was still there. I was shocked when I heard the M.C. announce "Put your hands together for Miss B. My mouth fell open. Was she a performer now? What was she going to do? I rushed out of the dressing room to see what she had up her sleeve. The music began to play as I saw her walk onto the stage. Rueben had recently won American Idol and had a hit single, "*Sorry, 2004*", and she lip-synced the words and performed the song like a pro. I was in awe, but my stubborn nature wouldn't let me be obvious. I stood back near the bar, but somehow her eyes found me and didn't let up. She finished the song and walked over to me. In her hand was a blue rose. "I'm sorry... I want to start over." She declared. I was secretly elated, but I couldn't outwardly show it. Now, although I was genuinely in love and wanted nothing more than to be one with her, I was terrified. Would I be setting myself up for disappointment again? A series of thoughts and emotions rushed through me. Excitement, curiosity, desire, and fear were among them, but the feeling that was most prominent was my all too real affinity and adoration for her. Though we'd only known each other for a short period, I'd learned things about her that made me want to be the one thing that she could rely on. I wanted to be the one to wash away all her pain. I wanted to show her that good women still existed and that she deserved that. I was drawn to her for far more than the physical. I believed we could be each other's missing piece.

We hugged and kissed, making our reconciliation official and much of the audience seemed to notice. That didn't matter to me. It felt like only she and I existed at that moment. I felt complete. We left the club together and spent the night making love in my bed. Every time she touched me it was like my feelings for her intensified. I hadn't realized it at the time, but my emotions were profoundly connected to the physical. Sex with her made it harder to detach and decipher the right or wrong things to do when it came to her. The next morning, she asked me to accompany her to her house. I agreed and got dressed. On the way, she vaguely explained her decision to end things with Mesha and said that she and her children would be moving out. I didn't want to pry, but I was thrilled and wanted to know when and how this would transpire. Maybe it was selfish of me, but I was eager to get this whole "Mesha" ordeal behind us. I was ready for us to start our life together. We pulled up to the brick bungalow, and B instructed me to wait in the car while she went in. I assumed that this was because Mesha was inside. It was no secret that B and I had been involved, but she still tried to maintain a certain level of respect and distance. I sat in the passenger seat, twiddling my thumbs, for all of ten minutes. Finally, B appeared inside the security door that adorned the front of her house and motioned for me to come in. I exited the car and walked up the porch steps. I opened the heavy gate and stepped inside. I wasn't sure what to expect, but I was prepared for whatever. I wasn't sure if there would be a verbal or physical confrontation, or if Mesha had simply left. Upon entering the house, at first, I heard and saw no one. It was early morning, so I assumed the children were in school and that Mesha wasn't there either. Suddenly I heard a woman crying coming from the rear of the house. I hesitated and then inched forward, trying to listen to the dialogue, if any.

Through a weepy voice, I heard Mesha say, "If this is what you want, fine." B didn't audibly respond before I saw Mesha appear in the hallway. As she looked at me, her eyes pierced through me, and she turned and walked into another room. I could faintly hear the commotion of her slamming things around as she packed. I stood still in the living room, not sure what to make of the situation. I could hear Mesha murmuring wishing I could make out her words. As her words became louder, I realized she was on a phone call.

"Can you just be on your way here?" She asked, demanding of the person on the other end. B came down the hallway, and she motioned for me to follow her outside. We got back into the car, and I couldn't help but to ask questions.

"What's going on? Is she moving out today? How did all this come about?" I quizzed.

"We haven't been right ever since that night you came over. I realized that I was in love with you and when she asked me I couldn't lie. She said she wasn't going to share me and so she was moving out." She explained.

"Oh, so you thought I would share you?" I questioned, not prepared for her response.

"Well, I was hoping..." she began. I shot her a look that said, "don't even finish that absurd ass thought" and she chuckled and laughed it off. I wondered if she was serious, but I decided not to pursue the issue. I was just excited about us finally having the chance to be together. I was nervous about the prospect of becoming a step-mom, but I was willing to fulfill whatever needs came with being her woman.

We sat in the car and talked for about thirty minutes when I saw a car pull in front of the house through the side view mirror. A tall, dark-skinned stud emerged from the driver's side and began walking toward the house. B took notice and got out of the car to address the approaching stranger.

"Can I help u?" I heard B ask.

"I'm here to help Mesha. She asked me to come." The woman responded, sizing B up. B reluctantly stood to the side and watched the stranger approach the porch. Mesha appeared in the doorway and held the door open, motioning for the woman to go in. The two of them shortly came out of the house with Mesha's possessions in hand and loaded them into Mesha's red minivan; the one B had gotten her as a gift that she practically threw back in her face. She honestly expressed that she didn't want that minivan and opted to drive B's sporty silver sedan instead, yet now she was loading her possessions into it. She and the stud packed what they could into the two vehicles and drove away without saying much else. At that point, B and I re-entered the house to assess what was to be the next step. When I'd initially went into the house, I was too busy being on guard to notice the magnitude of what this process would consist of, but I was quickly made aware. B had told me, prior, how Mesha's children had been destructive and caused extensive damage to her home, but that didn't prepare me for what I was witnessing now.

Chapter 31

The walls were painted a creepy, blood red, but looked as if the painter had abandoned the job halfway through. There was a huge gaping hole in the wall that separated the living room from the landing that led to the basement. On the adjacent wall, a hole had been plastered, almost identical in shape and size. It looked as if there had been a physical brawl and someone had been thrown through each orifice. The carpet, which I presume was once a shade of light grey, was now a murky, filthy brownish grey, caked with food and other residues. There was a faint odor of urine in the air and not much furniture stood in the front of the house. I followed her as we walked through, trying to figure out where to start.

"I want everything out. I'm starting fresh." She declared. I nodded in agreement as I couldn't see anything that could be salvaged. She turned to me and took me in her arms. "You're coming to live here with me, right?" she asked. Though I kind of figured that would eventually be the case, I was pleasantly surprised that she asked me formally. A huge smile rolled across my face as I nodded, happily agreeing to her rhetorical request. She kissed me, and that seemed to seal the deal. We stayed for much of that day, cleaning up and cleaning out. Virtually the entire latter portion of the front lawn was covered in discarded furniture and other effects that she had decided to dispose of. That afternoon, when it was time to pick Angelo up from head start, I decided I would have her drive me back to the apartment to retrieve some of my things. I still hadn't come up with a way to tell Corrine and Rae how serious things had quickly gotten between B and me, much less than I had planned to move in with her. Corrine and Rae had been kind of protective of me and especially when they got wind of how B had suddenly switched up on me. The Word was that Corrine was barely speaking to her at work. They had been relatively good friends it seemed until she started dating me. I loved Corrine and Rae, and I appreciated them stepping in and helping me when Tiny and I broke up. I valued their opinion, and I worried that they would judge me for moving so fast with B. I dreaded the impending conversation where I would have to tell them what I'd planned to do. I loved and respected them, but the truth of the matter was, I wanted a family of my own. I wanted what they had. I wanted a woman and a relationship to call mine.

I started up the apartment steps and sauntered to the door, with my heart feeling heavy. I opened the front door and Rae and Corrine were curled up on the couch, watching a movie.

"Hey mama and daddy," I greeted them, as I sometimes jokingly called them.

"Hey." They both seemed to reply in unison. I walked past them to my room, still wanting to avoid a lengthy conversation or questions that would force me to explain my reality. Once in my room, I threw a few essentials into an overnight bag and went back out into the living room.

"Well, you guys will have your apartment to yourselves again. I'm getting out of your hair." I said with a half of a smile, trying to make light of the situation. They both looked at each other, and then back at me, but didn't verbally respond. I wasn't sure what to think of the awkward silence until finally, Rae said, "So you're moving in, huh?"

Her tone didn't give away any emotion, so I was unsure how to answer her question. Corrine, on the other hand, didn't utter a word, neither did she make eye contact, which made me feel awkward. I guess my nervous energy stemmed from me not wanting to ruin our friendship by making such a hasty decision. Things had already been unusual between us, to say the least, that I didn't want this to ruin the chances of us gaining back some sense of normalcy. I knew they were suspicious of B, but I loved her and was determined to maintain peace in both situations. "I'll see u guys sometime tomorrow." I declared, walking out the door and downstairs to where B was waiting.

Chapter 32

M oving on from Rae and Corrine had been a smoother transition than I'd initially anticipated. They didn't give me grief about my quick process and seemed genuinely supportive. I still visited them regularly. Rae and I continued to hang out as we always had. I'd even recently pulled her in on the all-girl revue that I had been actively participating in, and L.J. was thrilled. Rae's beauty was a great addition to the show. There were a few other female exotic dancers on the show, but Rae had that little extra something. She infused an element of art and creativity to her striptease antics, almost like a classic burlesque performer. She had a beautiful body and great moves. The crowd loved her because she was more than just ass and tits.

Adjusting to the role of "mother" hadn't been so easy. I constantly tried to bond with Angelo, but my magic didn't seem to work on him the way it had with other kids. He just didn't seem to like me and would constantly ask B, "Mama, where's my other momma?" This caused me a lot of concern, and it made me question if we would ever become a family. I wondered how the three of us would have a future together if

Angelo didn't warm up to me. He was B's whole world and her only immediate family since her mother's untimely passing. Both of her parents died when she was a teenager, and she is still grief-stricken, especially over her mother. She'd even explained that her motivation behind becoming a mother was an attempt to fill that void, so Angelo was even more of a commodity. The experience of playing a role to my younger siblings was nothing compared to the trials that came with trying to be a mother figure to a toddler. I was immediately expected to fulfill every task that Mesha had concerning Angelo, and when I fell short, B harshly criticized me for it. I often got discouraged and questioned my abilities on a regular. I wondered if I would ever be good enough.

Growing up, physical punishment had always been a fixture in the way each of my parents disciplined us, so that was normal to me. B, on the other hand, didn't believe in spanking as a form of discipline, so when Angelo was disrespectful or got out of line, she hardly ever reacted. This bothered me. I was used to the tight ship that each of my parents ran, where back talk and blatant disrespect were grounds for an immediate ass whipping. One day, Angelo had been especially cranky and whiny; as a four-year-old can be from time to time. B was negotiating and pleading with him to behave and comply, and he would defiantly tell her, "No!" She did virtually nothing in the way of chastising him, and I was so irritated that before I knew it, I had snatched off my belt and commenced to give him what I felt he'd been long overdue for; an old-fashioned ass beating. She, of course, was furious and wasted no time letting me know it.

"You have no idea how to be a fucking parent! How the hell are you going to have me a fucking baby?!" she scolded me. I was speechless and heartbroken. I thought I was backing her up and standing with her as a united parental front when her son had been so disrespectful to her, and yet here she was ridiculing and belittling me for defending her. I was hurt and confused and had never felt so discouraged. I made a phone call to Rae and that night, I packed my things and left. I was not wanted there by her and certainly not by him.

This was now the second time that I'd felt cast to the side by the woman that I so desperately wanted to be with. I knew I wasn't perfect, by any means, but damn... did I deserve this? I didn't know what to do but run away. I felt unwanted and unwelcomed. I remembered feeling so abandoned when my mother would come home on her drunken rants and decide to put me out. Not before she fought me like I was someone on the street, though. I would find myself walking, sometimes at 3 or 4 in the morning, alone, aimlessly in the dark. Before long, I just started leaving on my own. Occasionally, my honorary Godparents would let me sleep over at their house. They were like family to me. Their daughter, Emily, and I were best friends in middle and high school, and they took me in and picked up where my parents lacked. Godfather or Paw as I affectionately called him, had connections in the music industry. He took me under his wing and started managing my early music career. He got me all kinds of studio equipment and taught me how to work it when I was just a teenager. He believed in me and my talent, but aside from that, he cared about me like one of his kids. I thought of him much like a dad as well. He was kind but protective, the way I felt a dad should be. I remember staying the night at their house and my sperm donor calling there to talk to me. I was stunned at what he had to say. He accused me of sleeping with my forty-year-old Godfather. I was floored and hurt. I couldn't understand at the time how he could even fathom such a thought about his fourteen-year-old daughter. But then this was the same man who had performed sexual acts with me, his daughter. Paw was always straight up with all of us kids, but never inappropriate. He loved us all like his own. Maybe my dad was just jealous of our relationship. He would always say some foul shit to me. He'd say explicit, inappropriate things that a father should never say to his child. I remember coming home from school one day when I was in fifth grade. Some rude boy had said to me and another girl that he wanted us to "suck him up." I ran home to my father upset and crying. I told him what that ingrate said to me, and he erupted in laughter. He said "don't worry. One day you'll step up to the "mike" and give your BEST performance." I didn't even know what that meant at the time, but the mere fact that he'd laughed when I was so hurt was enough to break me down. I cried incessantly. I was shocked at his reaction. I wanted him to go to that school and snap that boy's neck! I wanted him to defend and protect me. Instead, he broke my heart before any nigga had a chance to. Maybe that's why I never really attached feelings to any man. In my mind, none of them could be trusted.

B called relentlessly from the second I had packed up all my things to go back to Rae and Corrine's place, but I refused to answer. I just wasn't ready to talk to her yet. I felt so hurt and alone in that house with her and Angelo, who hated me so much. There was no point in going back there, primarily since I was now in competition with a toddler and his "other mother." In my eyes, there could be no resolve, so I sulked for a few days, not wanting to talk to anyone. Damn. I missed B like crazy, and I was for sure that I had fallen madly in love with her. So, when she called again, I answered.

"Why every time we disagree, you want to leave?" she asked. Truthfully, I didn't have a straight answer for that. There was no doubt she was what and who I wanted, but this whole motherhood concept and the harsh criticism that came with it terrified me. I wanted to be perfect in her eyes, and all she did was remind me how of great Mesha was with Angelo. It was downright demeaning how she insisted on informing me of how great the sex was between the two of them and how great of a cook Mesha was. I couldn't tell when we first met, but B could be cruel. It was clear that she had a painful past, but I couldn't understand for the life of me why she was so mean to me. Here I was trying to comfort her and show her that good women do exists, and she was punishing me for everything every other woman had done wrong. I was confused, yet I was still so in love with her. I saw things in her that I felt no one else did. Her softer side and her talents were things that not many people got to experience because she was so guarded. But when she lashed out, I was the one who felt her wrath. I was by no means perfect because when I felt hurt or attacked, my tongue could be a sword, but I was different with her. It was like my love for her wouldn't let me fight back, no matter how she violated me.

"I want you to come home." She declared. I was terrified. I felt like a failure around her and Angelo. I wanted so much to be perfect, and she made me feel as though I was severely lacking. Nevertheless, when she wanted me home, I didn't dare refuse. I got my things that night and went back to my woman. I was determined to get this stepmom thing down and do whatever else I needed to do to make them both happy. I wanted so much for it to work. Pretty soon, I found myself dressing a certain way. B had told me how she liked when Mesha wore cabbie hats. Soon I had a collection of cabbie hats. She also made it a point to let me know that she loved long, wavy hair. I was usually rocking a different hairstyle weekly, but I found myself almost always wearing long, wavy weaves. I even started wearing hazel contact lenses to make my eyes light like Mesha's. I longed to be loved by B just as much as she loved Mesha.

I transitioned into motherhood quickly, and I became very active. I went to every parent-teacher conference, carpooling, homework and field trips. I was very hands-on with all of Angelo's school activities as well as maintaining our household. Life was great, we were bonding as a family, and I couldn't be happier. B's work days were long, so it gave Angelo and I a lot of time to bond.

One evening, B came home from work and Angelo, and I was doing our nightly routine of homework, dinner, and bath. We were just finishing up when she pulled me into our bedroom. She sat me down on the bed, and I was about to be worried when she dropped down on one knee. She took a small silver box from her jacket pocket. She flipped the top open and held it out to me. I was stunned.

"Let's get married." She said. I kissed her at least a hundred times and couldn't contain my excitement. She put the beautiful, white gold and solitaire diamond ring on my finger. I had been waiting for this moment. All this time I had been questioning her love for me, but if she wanted me to be her wife, then she must be in love with me too, right? I was elated! I immediately started to plan our wedding. If she had said, she wanted to do it that day I would've jumped at the chance. She had made me the happiest I had ever been. I called Rae and told her the news. She seemed happy for me and shared the announcement with Corinne.

Later that night, Rae called back, but she didn't sound so good. I inquired what was wrong, and I could faintly hear Corinne's voice in the background, and she seemed excited or even angry.

"Corinne is angry at you for wanting to marry Brenda." She said.

"Why?" I asked, both disappointed and confused.

She's in love with you." Rae said flatly. I damn near dropped the phone. I was in shock. What? How? How could one of my closest friends be telling me that her girlfriend was in love with me? I'd just gotten engaged to the woman that I loved. This was insane. I was looking forward to them both sharing my special day. Things took a wrong turn, and once again, I was confused. "How? When? Where? Why now?" There was no way B could find this out. A threesome was out of the question.

Chapter 33

Over the coming weeks, things were incredibly awkward between Rae and me, even strained. I completely avoided even the idea of being around Corinne, as I was nervous, confused, and not even sure what to say. I wanted so badly for things to go back to the way they once were between the three of us. I hadn't had many people in my life that genuinely cared for me, but I believed they did. Rae was very dear to me mainly because she'd been my friend first. I know she only meant for the threesome to have a positive effect on their relationship, but it had backfired. I didn't want her to hate or be mad at me, but when I was around her, I felt the tension. Truthfully, I didn't want to be the cause of their break up. I wanted to see them in love and happy again, but I guess the damage had been done.

I tried to continue usually and move forward with my upcoming wedding. Since same-sex marriage wasn't legal in the U.S., we would have to go to Canada to be married. I got to work calling the Windsor City Hall to check the requirements and was able to obtain a list of chapels that performed same-sex marriage. I envisioned every aspect of our special day. I knew that I wanted to have a separate ceremony here in the states so that all of our family and friends could attend. I had been dreaming of my wedding day since childhood, and even though I didn't know at the time that I'd be marrying a woman, I knew I would marry the love of my life. I was madly in love with Brenda Wyatt and would have gone to the ends of the earth to show her. In conjunction with planning our wedding, I also began renovations to what would now be our house. Mesha's kids had done quite a number on the home that B's late mother had willed to her. From the holes in the walls to the irreparable damage to the carpet and floors, I started to dissect and restore. I enlisted the help of my cousin to do much of the repairs and painting, and B had someone in mind for the windows and floors. It was a little awkward when she told me that the person she was hiring was Mesha's uncle, but I went along with what my wife- to - be wanted. Uncle Elgin was an older man, about 50, and he seemed kind enough. He was tall, with a dark complexion and he walked with a bit of a limp. He spoke slowly with a southern accent and struck me as your typical, self-taught handyman. His work was phenomenal. The walls and paint were all coming together, and it wasn't long before I could hardly recognize the house from its previous state. One afternoon, I was home alone, and Elgin had come by to finish the kitchen and hallway floors. I had fallen asleep across our bed, and I awoke to Elgin standing over me. I was startled because the feeling of his breath on my face is literally what woke me. He had let himself into my room, and his lips were approximately four inches from mine. I woke up and gasped at the site of his face in much too close proximity to mine. I was sure that he was trying to perform some perverse act and I immediately jumped up and got as much space between us as I could. He laughed, but I didn't think shit was funny.

"What the hell are you doing?!" I demanded.

"Calm down. I didn't mean any harm," he said, in that southern drawl, still smiling. "I was just letting you know I was leaving is all." He continued. I was both confused and scared. I was there alone with him, and I didn't like the idea that he felt so comfortable invading my personal space. And what the hell was wrong with just knocking on my door and simply saying, from a few feet away, "Hey, I'm leaving." Something wasn't right with this dude, and I knew from that point on I wouldn't be left alone with him. When B got home, I immediately told her what he had done. She confronted him about it and he, of course, downplayed it as if I overreacted. Even if he hadn't had ill intentions, which I highly doubt, I still didn't see why it had been necessary for him to violate my personal space. It was inappropriate.

We had scheduled a shopping trip to look for what we would wear to Canada to be married. B had asked her gay dad, another stud named Anita, and her girlfriend to come along. I had met Anita previously through the first woman I'd dated. She and Tiffanie were friends, and she wasted no time hating on me to B and telling her about mine and

Tiffanie's bitter split. Of course, she made me out to be the crazy one, when the truth was she knew nothing about me. She'd met me once, and our interaction was limited. That didn't stop her from bad mouthing me to my fiancé and all the while being fake and pretending to be happy for us. She even had the nerve to pitch herself to me and offer to manage my singing career. It was laughable considering she was a barber and had zero connects or even knowledge of the business. Nothing ever came of the arrangement, and I was always giving her shady ass the side eye. Her girlfriend seemed cool enough, and she and I made small talk while our studs bonded over shopping. We visited a few stores, and though we were looking for something simple just to go to Canada, I still wanted to look and feel special on the day I would officially become Mrs. Brenda Wyatt. I couldn't find anything that gave me that feeling and B became frustrated with me. We parted ways with the other couple, and she wasted no time on the drive home scolding me.

"Why do you always have to make things so complicated?!" she asked, the disdain apparent in her voice. I was a little put-off and didn't understand why she was so upset, but by then I was used to being harshly criticized when it came to B.

I was immediately defensive. "It's my wedding day too! I should be able to look how I want to look!" I retorted, becoming more upset by her reaction.

"The shit isn't even that serious!" she scoffed.

"Oh. So now our wedding isn't serious?! It's all a big fucking joke to you, huh?!" I exclaimed, twisting her words.

"You're fucking tripping." She replied, rolling her eyes in disapproval. With each word she said, I was more upset and convinced that she was picking an argument because she didn't want to go through with marrying me. I was huffing and puffing by this time, and the debate continued as we reached home.

"Well if that's the way you feel about it maybe we should just call the whole thing off. Since it's no big deal to you anyway, fuck it!" I yelled angrily. We'd come in the house by then, and Angelo was in earshot in the room next to ours.

"Fuck it then. I don't give a fuck." She said, shrugging her shoulders nonchalantly. I was so enraged with emotions that I threw the contents of an unfinished glass of wine sitting on the nightstand in her face. I then threw the empty glass at the wall behind her, shattering it onto the floor. In quick succession, she picked up the bottle that the glass of wine had been poured from and attempted to hand it to me. I looked at her, confused.

"GO AHEAD! HIT ME BITCH! TAKE THE BOTTLE, BITCH and HIT ME! That's what you want to do, right?!" she yelled, still practically shoving the bottle into my hands. I was stunned. Why would she think I'd want to hit her? And why would she think I would want to hit her with a glass bottle? Even when Angela and I had been together and had a fight, we never used the word bitch. That was something that was just off limits. Not only was it shocking to hear this from the woman I loved so deeply, but it stung... and bad. It hurt as bad as it had when my mother said it to me as a child. I just stood there, not sure how to react. After an awkward silence, I could hear Angelo crying in the next room. B immediately ran to his aid. I followed her to make sure he was fine. I stood in the doorway, not sure how to proceed, as she held and tried to comfort him. "This wedding and this whole relationship is off!" she declared angrily. I turned around and went back to the room we shared. I immediately started packing my things. It was clear I was disposable to her, and I wasn't going to grant her the satisfaction of throwing me out on the street. I didn't want to leave. I loved her more than life, and I wanted her to love and value me. I did everything within my power to be perfect for her. Why couldn't she see what she had in me? I didn't call Rae that night as I usually did. I know they were probably growing tired of me and my drama. I felt bad. I hated dragging other people into my problems. Since B had brought Angelo into our bed to sleep with her, I stayed in his room, but I didn't get much sleep. I tossed, turned, cried, and wracked my brain as to how I was going to fix this situation. After all, it had been me that had initiated the breaking of our engagement. I wanted to marry B more than anything but when I felt attacked; I had a habit of running and shutting down. In hindsight,

I wished I had been more rational and just talked through our disagreement. Now the woman I loved was looking at me differently.

Over the next few days, I avoided being home as much as possible. When I was there, I retreated to Angelo's room and isolated myself. I felt terrible and didn't want to face B, yet I wanted so much for us to work things out. She was just so angry I was afraid and didn't know how to approach her. My pride and my walls wouldn't allow me to appear vulnerable, however. I played hard and continued the silent treatment for days. When I was hurt or emotional, I could be as stubborn as a mule. I didn't dare show any sign of weakness, but as soon as I was alone with my thoughts, I would cry my eyes out. I missed my precious B. I was terrified at the thought of losing her. I shuddered at the thought of being without the family that I'd worked so hard to fit into. After nearly a week of literally looking past each other, I spoke up. "Are we going to talk about this?" I asked, still subconsciously keeping my guard up.

"What's there to talk about?" she asked, rhetorically.

"We need to talk about our relationship and impending marriage," I answered, feeling that familiar lump in my throat.

"You called OFF our wedding. Remember?" She reminded me.

"I said maybe we shouldn't because you made me feel like I was such an aggravation to you and that you didn't want to go through with it," I argued.

"Well, now I don't!" she said, abruptly. I was crushed, but I'd quickly learned that trying to reason with her when she was angry was a losing battle. It was clear that she was furious with me, but did she not want to marry me? I was hurt and confused. I didn't want to upset her more, but I wanted us to just get back to planning our future. I wanted desperately just to make her laugh, and we forget this whole thing ever happened. I wanted to fall back into her arms and tell her how sorry I was and that I loved her more than anything. I knew I had to get us back right... but how? I had to find a way. I knew I didn't want to be without her... ever.

Things went on like this for weeks, and I was dying inside. Although we were still under the same roof, she was barely speaking to me. She didn't seem as angry anymore, but things were not the same. I tried to continue regularly, and I decided to focus my attention on other things. I made sure that I kept up with my duties as the woman of the household so that B wouldn't lose sight of the fact that I was wife material. I wanted her to see that in spite of our argument, I still wanted and deserved to be Mrs. Wyatt. One evening I heard B's keys unlocking the front door, and I got excited as I usually did when she came home. Even though we still hadn't reinstated our engagement, I was still very much in love with her, and I was hopeful that things would blow over. I heard her call my name from the living room and I poked my head out of the bedroom door to answer. She smiled when she saw me, and she hadn't done that in forever.

I was happy and worried at the same time. This was such a change from how she'd looked at me for the past month, and I wasn't sure what to make of it.

"I bought you something." She finally said. I was shocked. She'd been so upset with me for so long, and I was starting to wonder if things would ever be the same and now she'd gotten me a gift? I wondered what it could be. "Come outside." She instructed. I followed her out onto the front porch. In the driveway was a white Chrysler Dynasty. I was outdone, she bought me a car? I was confused, but I was ecstatic and grateful. I'd been without a vehicle since Angela had decided to be spiteful and take the car she'd given me back. I got around pretty well, considering, but there's nothing quite like having your own. I turned to her and threw my arms around her neck and hugged her.

"Thank you, so much, baby. You're the best!" I told her, planting a kiss on her lips. I'd been happy with her just talking and laughing with me and here it was she was buying me gifts? I felt confident then that we were well on our way to being back where we needed to be. Though she hadn't mentioned the engagement or the wedding, the fact that she thought enough of me to buy me my whip had to mean that she planned on being with me long term.

Things were going well with business, and the renovation of the house was coming along nicely. Nicara had just purchased a home and was doing some remodeling of her own, so I was grateful that she shared some of her DIY tips with me. I had a knack for that kind of thing anyway. Ironically, though I was the femme in the relationship, I was handier than B. I had quite a few masculine tendencies as a result of being on my own early in life. I learned quickly that you couldn't wait or depend on anyone. If you want something done, be prepared to do it yourself. Although we'd hired people to perform specific tasks, I had my hands in most of the household projects. Carpentry and craftsmanship weren't precisely B's forte, so she didn't seem to mind when I took the lead. I was doing everything from drywall and painting to laying carpet and hanging light fixtures, and our kingdom was taking shape. I was finally feeling more comfortable as the woman of the house.

I called my little sister Nyema one evening to come over and babysit Angelo so that B and I could have a night out. I'd talked to her earlier while I was at work and she told me that she'd gotten tickets to a concert at the Fox Theater. She mentioned who would be playing, but I didn't care who it was as long as I got to spend some quality, alone time with her. My day ran long, and I was sure that I would have to be in a mad rush to get ready in time for the concert, but I was up for the challenge. I left the salon and headed to the east side to pick up Nyema. It took us about forty more minutes to return to the west side, and I knew I would hear about my being late from B. I rushed into the house, fully prepared to take whatever she had to dish out, but to my surprise, the house was still. I walked from room to room looking for B and Angelo, but they weren't there. I fished for my cell phone to call her. Maybe she had gone to gas up the car or get something at the last minute. I dialed her, but her phone went to voicemail. I hung up and dialed again, but was still prompted to leave a message, so I did.

"Baby I'm at the house. Where you at? Call me." I recorded. I waited, but she didn't return my call. I called at least four more times and still got no answer. I'd started to worry when my phone rang.

"Hello, I frantically inquired. "You called?" she asked flatly. I could barely hear her words over the loud music playing in the background.

"Where are you at?" I asked, my concern shifting to anger.

"I'm at the concert." She answered, nonchalantly.

"You're at the concert? You went without me?!" I asked, now hurt and angry.

"I got to go. I'll see you later." She said abruptly and hung up on me. I looked at the phone in disbelief. I was angry and hurt. Why would she go without me? I'd been looking forward to us positively interacting for weeks, and she goes out without me? I was furious! I wanted to cry and tear some shit up at the same time. I reached for my keys and purse and instructed Nyema to follow. There was no way I was going to sit at home and cry tonight while B was out having the time of her life. I was pissed and needed to blow off some steam. We headed to City Heat Gentleman's Club since it was practically around the corner from the house. Nyema was now 19 so she could hang with me and get into the clubs. We drank like a fish and watched the girls do pole tricks until two a.m. We left the club and headed to the house, and though intoxicated, my blood was still boiling from being left behind earlier. I staggered into the house and headed for the bedroom. B's car was in the driveway, so I knew I'd find her there. I turned on the light and started in on her.

"Why the FUCK would you go to that concert without me?! Who the fuck did you go with?!" I demanded.

"I went by myself. Don't come in here yelling and questioning me. I invited you, but your inconsiderate ass wasn't here, so I left!" she snapped. I was stifled, yet still on fire. I didn't believe for one second that she'd gone to that concert alone. She was still dressed up in what I assume she'd worn out that night and I could still smell the Gautier cologne from across the room, and it fueled my anger even more.

"I had to fucking work! I guess that guess that was just your way of saying fuck me, huh! What? Did you and that bitch reconcile?!" I barked. She snickered and turned her back to me.

"Your motherfucking ass should've been where you needed to be. I'm through talking." She coldly declared. I was speechless. I wanted just to slap her. How could she be so heartless? It was only a few weeks ago she'd been so kind and bought me a car, and now she was acting like I meant nothing to her? I was starting to feel like I didn't know whether I was coming or going when it came to her. Things were so unpredictable when it came to "US." One minute we would be kissing, and in love and the next we'd be arguing. She could be so cruel. Accurate enough, I could be overly emotional, but it was because I didn't know how to handle how she sometimes totally disregarded me and our relationship. At times, she seemed to have no emotion at all when it came to me other than anger. I was starting to get discouraged. I was never really the jealous or insecure type, but I'd begun to suspect that she was still interacting with Mesha. In spite of my suspicion, I agreed when she said that she even wanted to maintain a relationship with her kids. If there had been any inappropriate dealings between the two of them, the children hadn't been at fault, so I wasn't about to take my frustration out on them. Mesha's oldest son was especially close to B, so when he and his mother's new girlfriend weren't getting along, he asked if he could stay with us. I didn't hesitate to agree, as I was determined to keep my disdain for their mother a separate matter from the children. I too had come from a chaotic upbringing, so my heart went out to them in that way. Robert was fourteen and, to my surprise, was very respectful and sweet. I'm sure it had been told to him that I'd been the sole reason for the breakup of their family, but he never reacted negatively toward me. He was smart and mature, so maybe he just knew his mother was full of shit.

Robert settled into his new living environment effortlessly, and we got along just fine. I treated him like a younger brother, and he didn't seem to mind when I required things of him around the house. He was always very respectful and even delightful to be around. Angelo was somewhat of a different story. He was defiant and resistant to me at times. However, he seemed to be slightly adjusting. He'd have his moments, mainly when B was around. I'd hear him asking her about Mesha and if she was coming back, and that hurt me. I wanted him to hold ME in that regard. Robert, on the other hand, didn't seem to mind at all that his mother wasn't around. He'd, sometimes, go to visit her on the weekends but he rarely mentioned her at home.

B had come home from work one evening with shopping bags in hand. She sat the bags on the bed and began to pull out the contents of each one. One contained dinner from the Olive Garden; the other held candles, bubble bath, baby oil and matching pajamas for she and I. There was a pant set for her and a gown for me, both with matching prints. It seemed she'd had a romantic evening in mind since both boys were away for the weekend. She drew us a bath, and after we ate dinner, we soaked in the tub together. We kissed and washed each other's backs, and I was in a state of bliss. I loved this woman so much, and I wanted so much for us to get back to a good place. We got out of the tub and dried off; slipping into the new silk pajamas B had gotten for us. I went to the kitchen and got a glass of wine, as I had switched from drinking liquor in an attempt to steady myself from my addictive behavior when it came to alcohol. B wasn't much of a drinker and would always give me the side eye when I wanted to have a drink. I started drinking wine, thinking it would be less of a turn off to her. She was a weed smoker, and I never judged her for it. Even though I was never a smoker, I figured everyone has a vice and who was I to turn up my nose to hers? In fact, I liked who she became when she smoked. She was sweet and kind and affectionate, and I found myself almost wanting her to.

I sipped my wine as she smoked her blunt and soon we were both feeling the effects. She finished off the pasta she'd ordered, and I began to gulp the wine I once sipped. This was the best evening we'd had in a long time and I was looking forward to the lovemaking that I was sure would follow. I was considerably tipsy at this point, and it had gotten late, so when B's cell phone rang it startled me. She looked at the caller I.D. display and abruptly flipped the phone closed. My antennae went up, but I didn't say anything. I continued to drink while I could see her trying to pretend that phone call didn't take place. I'd been increasingly suspicious in the previous weeks, so this late-night phone call put me on edge. The cell phone lit up again, but this time, there was no sound. My suspicion quickly shifted to anger, and the alcohol just fueled it.

"Who the fuck is that and WHY did you put it on silent?!" I demanded. She shook her head and chuckled a little. I found nothing funny and her utter disregard for my feelings started to arouse a familiar feeling. The phone lit up again, and before she could react, I snatched it from her hand. She lunged at me, and we began to tussle. She started trying to pry my fingers away from the phone, but they were tightly clasped. I knew she'd allow me to do what I so desperately wanted to, which was the answer, so I tried to make a run for the bedroom door. She caught up with me and wrestled me down again, this time successfully taking the phone away from me.

"Your silly ass BITCH!" she snarled. I immediately felt both my eyes well up, and my blood begins to boil. I just stood there in the doorway as she nonchalantly sat back down on the bed and glued her eyes to the T.V. Why was she so cruel to me and more importantly, why was I allowing it? I didn't have an answer, and I was inconsolable. I felt the tears fall and I just wasn't in the mood to give her the satisfaction of seeing my cry while she showed no emotion at all, so I grabbed my keys and purse and headed for the door. I jumped in my car with no destination in mind. I just knew I didn't want to be there. I started the car, and the alcohol-fueled anger overwhelmed me. I was hurt and furious.

Chapter 34

I drove off into the night, fast and recklessly down the street. I only got to the end of the block when I tried to make a left turn and lost control of the car. I crashed through the guardrail at the edge of the field at Ford High School. The airbag deployed, saving me from flying through the windshield, but knocking the wind from me. Smoke filled the car, and everything went black. I'm not sure how much time lapsed, but I awoke to the chaos around me. The flashing red lights illuminated the dark field, and the smoke still stung my eyes. A man stood over me with a thick chain leash attached to a colossal pit bull dog. I was terrified of pit bulls but when I tried to move, I couldn't. I lay there in the field, unable to even talk. I could see the E.M.T. crew moving swiftly around me, but it hurt me even to breathe. Faintly, I could hear B's voice in the distance. She was running toward me when a burly, male paramedic stopped her. "Whoa..." I could hear him say. "Who are you, ma'am? Do you know her?" he questioned.

"YES. She lives with me!" she answered, with excitement apparent in her voice, as she tried again to rush past him. Just then, two more techs situated me on a board and proceeded to load me onto a stretcher, wedging my head between splints, preventing me from hearing much of the remainder of their conversation.

On the way to the hospital, I wondered what was happening with B and me. How did we end up here? I was lying on the stretcher wondering about our life together. As much physical pain as I was in, the pain in my heart ached much worse. Had she been cheating on me the whole time? Did she even love me at all? The tears began to flow and didn't stop. What should've been a ten-minute ride to Sinai Grace Hospital seemed like a road trip out of town. My heart was so heavy, and that familiar feeling of wanting to give up on everything was looming again. I was just so tired of the constant disappointment. What had I done to deserve such misery and sorrow? I didn't know, but the shit was getting old. I got to the E.R. and was met by Rae and Corrine. Rae waited in an exam room with me while Corrine stayed in the lobby. Rae began to ask me questions but didn't want to pry. I gave her a vague version of the night events, and she didn't give much of a response. It still hurt to talk and there was an extreme burning sensation around my throat. I was afraid to touch it, but I had to know what was causing this feeling. I reached up and touched my neck, and I was startled when it felt wet. I looked at my fingers, and there were blood and puss. The airbag had severely burned my neck and face. I hadn't yet looked into a mirror, but I panicked and began to cry.

"It's not that bad. Don't cry." Rae tried to comfort me. I was inconsolable. Not only did I imagine a horrible facial disfiguration, but I felt this fairytale picture I had in my mind fading. The "happily ever after" that I so desperately wanted with B may not ever come to pass and I was both afraid and despondent. I wanted so much to be everything she wanted, but it seemed no matter how hard I tried, she'd find a way to make me feel inadequate.

After being evaluated by what seemed like at least twenty different doctors and after multiple x-rays and scans, the decision was made that I would be discharged. The fact that I no longer had medical insurance, I'm sure, helped render the said decision, and I was informed that I was free to go. Because I was still very sore, Rae helped me dress, and she took instruction on how to change the dressings on my neck and face. She helped me out to her car where Corrine was waiting. On the way home, Corrine wasted no time telling me of her loathing for B and how I would be a fool to go back there. Maybe she was right. Perhaps I was a fool. After everything we'd been through in our short time together, I should've been running to the nearest exit, yet I still loved her and wanted her to love me.

She hadn't even bothered to show up to the hospital to check on me, yet I wanted to get back to her. Though the thought of their criticism made me cringe, I reluctantly requested for them to drive me back there. Corrine silently shook her head and did what I'd asked.

When we pulled up to the house, to my surprise, B was waiting out front. The car wasn't in the "park" position when Rae flung open the passenger door and leaped from it. Before any of us could react, she lunged at B, going straight for her face with closed fists. Corrine quickly threw the car in park and hurriedly ran to try and pry Rae off of B. I exited the car as fast as my sore body would allow me to and tried to get between the two of them. I didn't want to see the two of them fighting, but I understood my friend's rage. They'd watched in horror as this woman treated me like crap for nearly six months and now they'd sat with me in the hospital while she was nowhere in sight. As fucked up as the situation was, I was grateful to have people who cared enough to defend my honor. After Corrine successfully restrained Rae and told B a few choice words of her own, they left. I was still hurting, both physically and emotionally, and I just wanted to lie down and sleep.

I awoke the next morning alone, even sorer than the night before. The house was still, and I was still confused as to what could have taken place. I got up and went to the bathroom and peered at myself in the mirror. I felt my eyes well up. I was visibly battered from the crash, but even more emotionally from my fragmented relationship. I was so unhappy, and I had no idea how to fix it. I removed the gauze dressing that encircled my still stinging neck. The skin around my neck and jaw was reddish purple and oozing. I couldn't stand to look at it, so I hurriedly washed the area and put a fresh gauze bandage on to cover it. I lay back in the bed and turned on the T.V. to distract myself. My cell phone began to buzz. It was B, but I didn't feel like talking. I looked at the display, and it read "6 missed calls" all from B. It was clear that she had a message that she wanted to relay, but I was in no mood to hear it. I then received a text message, but I didn't read it either, nor did I respond.

I drifted in and out of sleep for much of the day, and I awoke to the sound of B's keys unlocking the front door. When I could hear her footsteps getting closer, I quickly sat up to fix my disheveled appearance.

"I've been calling you." she declared, poking her head into the bedroom door. "I've been asleep most of the day," I answered, wanting to avoid the conversation. Even though I was so sad, I still couldn't deny that I loved and wanted this woman more than life. The thought of being without her terrified me, yet the prospect of being with her started to terrify me. She knew how to hurt me and wasn't afraid to use those tactics any time she saw fit. Still, I wanted to be her wife, and I wanted to be perfect for her. My mind constantly raced with questions of how I could be better and how I could make her love me the way that I loved her. It was clear that she didn't from the way that she constantly criticized me and how she made it painfully apparent that her attention was being divided. I wondered how I could make her see me the way I saw her. I wanted her to be madly in love with me and see no other woman but me. I made changes to myself the way she liked, almost always. I was convinced that there was something I lacked that she wanted or needed in a woman and I was determined to find out what it was and fix it. "They towed your car," she interjected, jarring me from my wandering thoughts. I didn't respond. I honestly didn't care what happened to the car. All I wanted was B.

I tried for weeks not to let the slump I was in show. I kept up with my wifely routine as best as I could, but inside I was sad and confused. Ironically, B's behavior toward me seemed different. There were no more late night anonymous phone calls, and she was much more attentive than she'd been over the past few months. She was affectionate and sweet, and we made love on a regular basis. Even with all of her newfound affinity for me, I was still always on edge, waiting for the next time she would switch up. My trust for her had faded almost entirely. I tried for weeks to shake my somber mood but to no avail. B didn't seem to notice that I wasn't myself. Maybe she didn't care. I still wondered if our relationship would ever progress because B made no mention of our engagement or wedding. Maybe making me her wife wasn't what she had in mind at all. The thought of this saddened me, and I wasn't sure how to turn things around. Then I had an idea. I woke up early one morning and hopped a cab to Hamtramck. I got to Joseph Campau and Caniff and exited the cab. I walked about two blocks and found what I was looking for.

"Hello... May I help you?" a middle-aged, Bangladeshi gentleman inquired.

"Yes. I'm looking for a men's band in yellow gold with diamonds." I declared. The salesman motioned for me to come to a display case at the rear of the store. There was a wide selection of jewelry to choose from. Everything from pendants to earrings to bridal ensembles and the styles all varied. I knew B preferred yellow gold, whereas I preferred white, so my eyes were immediately trained on a thick yellow gold band with a white gold overlay, dripping in brilliant Baguette diamonds. It was gorgeous and perfect. The salesman handed it to me, and it was even more stunning up close.

"It costs twelve hundred dollars," he advised me.

"Is there layaway available?" I inquired.

"Sure," he answered, explaining the terms. I gave him a down payment of five hundred dollars and was to return within a few weeks with the balance. I returned the following week and retrieved the ring. If this didn't let her know how dangerous I was, I didn't know what would.

That evening, it surprised me when B came home early and sat down next to me on the bed. It always made me nervous when she wanted to talk, as I was not sure if what she had to say would be good or bad. I held my breath and listened.

"I've been thinking, and I don't want to wait to get married," she said. We can go to Canada and do it Friday." she announced. I was stunned. I was almost sure that marrying me was the last thing on her mind and here she wanted to do it in less than a week? She pulled a large knot of money from her pocket and gave me a handful of bills. "Go shopping baby. Find us something nice to wear," she instructed. My shock turned to bliss, and I took her face in my hands and kissed her. I had planned to present her with the ring, but this revelation made the moment even sweeter.

"I love it!" she exclaimed, as I slipped the ring onto her finger. All of the worry and depression I had felt fell away, and I was elated. Maybe I would get my fairytale after all.

I wasted no time preparing. I found a beautiful, form-fitting cream-colored gown. It was floor length and hugged in all the right places. It was simple, yet beautiful and elegant. I found a cream colored, tailored pin-striped suit for my love. It was, technically, a woman's suit, but had just enough of a masculine touch. Nothing about B's frame was masculine, so she still needed something that would fit her curves properly. I'd made arrangements for us to go and obtain the marriage license from city hall, as there would be a twenty-four-hour waiting period before we could be married. We went that Friday as planned and applied for our marriage license. It was surreal as I came one step closer to being Mrs. Brenda Wyatt. We waited one full week to prepare for our nuptials. I was nervous, and I could tell that my wife- to- be was too. Though the wedding was to be small and intimate, only about ten people, I still felt all the anxiety that any other bride would. I'd called my favorite cousin DeJuana and my kid sister Nyema to accompany me and had even decided I'd let my sperm donor walk me down the aisle. It was amazing how I could even stomach a man who'd brutalized me in every way imaginable; much less allow him to be a part of something that meant so much to me. He seemed, in recent time, to be attempting to establish a relationship with me, though at the time I was blind to his motives. With him, there was always a motive. B had invited her longtime friend, Ginelle to accompany her because she didn't have many blood relatives. I called my mother and told her of my plans, but she expressed no interest in attending. I guess I wasn't shocked at her blankness, but deep down it still hurt. Even if I weren't marrying a man, it would've been nice to have my mother's support. Regardless, nothing was going to stop me from marrying the woman of my dreams.

B and I had decided to follow the tradition and not see each other on that day before the actual time of the wedding. She left early for work as usual but decided she would get ready at Ginelle's. I spent the morning at the salon, getting gorgeous and preparing for my big moment. I'd decided I would wear my hair in an elegant bun. I didn't want to wear a veil and wanted my face and shoulders to be accentuated. I joked around with my co-workers as I put the finishing touches on my hair and makeup. I hadn't told any of them until that morning that B and I were getting married that day.

"Well, I mean, to each his own..." one of the girls said as if I needed her seal of approval."

"So, you're going to marry her?" another inquired. They all knew my orientation, but I was well aware that heterosexual people don't take gays seriously, so it didn't surprise me that they had so many questions. I mostly shrugged everyone off and continued to finish off my look. Once I was satisfied with my hair and makeup, I headed to DeJuana's and then east to pick up my sperm donor and Nyema. With my family in tow, I headed for the tunnel to Canada.

The succession of motorists at the tunnel entrance was astronomical as usual. After a miserably long wait, we were finally up to get through the Border Patrol Security. A prudish, tight-faced white female officer approached the car.

"I need to see everyone's proof of citizenship." she almost demanded. We all pulled out our various forms of identification and handed it to her. After verifying each of us, she handed back our I.D.'s.

"Pull over to the side, please. We need to inspect this vehicle". She declared, saying something inaudible into the small radio clipped to her upper chest.

"Why?" I asked the irritation in my voice apparent.

"Pull over to the side please!" she repeated sternly. I did and pulled over to the designated area as the officer followed on foot. "I need everyone to step out of the vehicle and stand over there against the wall." She instructed. In a million times I'd been to Canada, I had never been searched and treated like a criminal, and on today they pull this shit. I was furious! A male officer had walked over and exchanged a few words with the officer who'd flagged us.

"What are you going to Canada for today?" the female officer asked. I looked down at the white gown I was wearing and answered in the most sarcastic and condescending tone I could muster.

"I'm getting married, and you're making me late!" Then I rolled my eyes at her so hard it gave me a headache.

"We'll need to search the vehicle," she repeated, apparently trying to intimidate me. I had nothing to hide, so her efforts were in vain. She and the burly white male officer began searching the car. It was B's car, and I said a silent prayer that she hadn't left a tail in the ashtray. Just then, another officer sauntered over, walking a large black Labrador retriever. What the hell?! I was on fire by now as the three of them were apparently having a field day sifting through the contents of my trunk.

"Do you have anything to declare?" the bitchy female officer asked sarcastically.

"My fiancé's wedding ring," I answered flatly, handing her the velvet box that held B's ring.

"WIFE- to- be?" she asked, looking both shocked and offended.

"That's right!" I retorted, almost daring her to challenge me. I was pissed! I was envisioning myself running into her somewhere out of uniform and wearing her ignorant ass out. I was jolted from my officer ass- whipping fantasy by a wet nose sniffing my hand. The younger male officer with the dog had walked all up in my space. He allowed the dog to "inspect" me for a few uncomfortable moments and then he'd moved on to my father. The dog sniffed my father and then sat down. The dog alerted on the gentleman, and he informed the other officers. I was pretty sure that my father had long since given up weed and cigarettes as he had a heart condition that impaired his breathing, but this dog was saying different. Then he moved on to my cousin, an avid weed smoker and the dog walked right past her. If this wasn't the biggest heap of bullshit, I didn't know what was. They carried on this bogus "inspection" for another forty-five minutes before finally letting us go. When I got back into the car, I had five missed calls from B and three voicemails.

"Where are you?" one of them demanded. I hurried through the tunnel and finally emerged into Windsor. I found the church, located on Assumption Road and parked the car. I retrieved my bouquet from the trunk, and we scrambled inside. A fair skinned woman with salt and pepper hair and a thick, Trinidadian accent greeted us.

"I am Sharon, the minister," she informed us. "Brenda is here already on the block." She led us into the sanctuary where the wedding would take place. I informed her that I would be making an entrance and walking the aisle just like in a traditional marriage and that I would need a mike. She handed me a cordless microphone and directed my father and me to the sanctuary entrance. It was go time!

Positioned at the doors of the chapel, we began the wedding march. "Some people live for the fortune... Some people live just for the fame," I began to sing. The butterflies were doing somersaults as I walked toward my love. My eyes welled up, and my voice began to tremble a little with anxiety. I was determined to sing past the huge lump in my throat, so I began to belt a little louder. B looked amazing in the white suit as she nervously flashed me a smile. "Some people want it all, but I don't want nothing at all... If it ain't you baby..." I sang to her. Those words couldn't have been more accurate if I'd written them myself. I didn't want to live life if I couldn't have B in it with me. I was so emotional. I wanted to scream from the rooftops as I became Mrs. Brenda Wyatt! I finished the song, and when prompted by the minister, B read the vows she'd written for me, promising to love me and be my teammate in everything for life, and I wholeheartedly believed her.

"Do you take this woman to be your lawful partner in life?" the minister asked me. "Yes! I DO." I declared.

She posed the same question to B, and she answered, "I do." "By the power vested in me by the Province of Windsor/ Ontario, I now pronounce you partners in life! You may seal your union." the minister announced. B and I shared a passionate kiss, and I was officially Mrs. Wyatt! I was ecstatic.

We stayed behind for a few moments to sign off on the paperwork and then took some pictures. Ginelle had captured the entire wedding on her camcorder, but I never got to watch the footage. We left the church and crossed back over to the U.S. without incident. We dropped off my cousin and sperm donor and B, Nyema and I headed to Baker's lounge for a celebratory dinner and Jazz. We ate and enjoyed the sultry music and were congratulated by the M.C. and a few audience members at our wedding. My wife looked so good I couldn't wait to drop off my kid sister and get home to consummate! The sex that night was steamy and passionate. It seemed as if B was much more into me that she had ever been. We were kissing and touching each other the way we never had, it seemed. She was even more uninhibited. She'd let me eat her before, but this night she almost begged for it. As I licked and sucked on her, she exploded time after time, and it was terrific. She gripped my hair and pulled me in closer until I was almost at a loss for air. I didn't mind because she was my wife and she tasted better than ever. She enjoyed it just as much when I rode her face. She locked her forearms on my thighs, preventing me from doing anything but grinding on her soft lips. Just as I thought I would pass out, she stopped and put on her secret weapon and made me cum at least four more times. Man, that woman slang dick like she was born with it! She should teach a class. Men included. She gripped my shoulders as she hit me from behind and had me singing her name. We made love for hours that night. I was never happier. I was so in love and for the first time, I officially belonged to someone. I belonged to the love of my life, and she was the woman of my dreams. She had her flaws, but she was perfect in my eyes. I understood her. I knew that pain created certain defenses and behaviors in people and I was determined to stick by her and help her through. I wanted so much to be the one to heal her broken heart, but I was oblivious to the fact that I needed healing.

We carried on our newlywed bliss for weeks. We didn't take a honeymoon but was summer, so we did take Angelo to Cedar Point for a weekend. B's job was still pretty demanding of her, and she didn't feel comfortable taking an extended vacation and being away from her store for an extended period. We were still developing the renovations to the house, and there were just too many things going on to abandon ship. Our house was coming along beautifully. We'd redone the floors throughout, and all of the walls had been repaired and adorned with fresh, vibrant paint. I'd done window treatments through the house as well, and we'd installed all new stainless appliances. I took on Angelo's room as a unique project. I painted it a vivid Sea Blue and bought him a bright red, offset bunk bed with a full- sized bed on the bottom. I included a beautiful table and chairs set and also a desk for him to do his homework on. I finished the ensemble with a beautiful television set and organized the closet with all the new clothes and shoes I'd bought for him. Life was great, and I was incredibly grateful for my new family. Robert was still there with us, but it was up in the air whether he would return home to his mother. He'd begun spending more time at her house, and from what I understood, she and her recent love interest had broken up. It had been the relationship of his mother that caused him to want to come and stay with us, to begin with. I liked having Robert around. He was a sweet and respectful kid, and he loved Angelo. He helped out tremendously when it came to him, and I had no complaints with him. B and I were not only getting along, but we were seriously into each other. We were all over each other, in fact. We were always kissing and holding hands in public, and we sneaked off and made out every chance we got. We fucked like rabbits for months. It almost blinded me to any of the other goings on around me. Never had I been so enthralled with any person or thing. Whatever she asked, I did and even the things she didn't. I was gone.

My father was uncomfortably close in the months after we were married. I was always suspicious of him, but I couldn't help longing for a relationship with my dad, so I allowed him in against what my gut was telling me. He was always asking to come over for days at a time and had even forged a relationship with my stepson. I was pretty sure that he preferred little girls, but I was still leery of letting him be alone with Angelo. You can never be sure with pedophiles, and he was a known pedophile. It seemed as though he was looking to benefit in some way, but I tried only to see the good in the situation. B seemed to take to him and enjoy having him around. I guessed that she just missed having parents herself, so he, kind of, reminded her of what it was like. My mother had met B and Angelo, but never expressed interest in developing a relationship with either of them. I can imagine that this bothered B as the maternal interaction was a clear and apparent void in her life. She always cried and grieved for her mother, even though she had passed over a decade ago. It was like the pain was still fresh. I didn't understand what she felt as far as that and how alone she felt, even with all the love and support I thought I was offering her. No matter how I smothered her, it seemed as if she was always detached in some way and I would have to experience it myself to get it.

B and I began to bond in every way as a married couple. We spent all of our spare time virtually together, working on our house and building our family foundation. We went on lots of dates, and she even started to perform with me at my gigs. Together we came up with one creative production after another and appeared on stage together as studsband and wife. I felt so alive, and for the first time, I felt real definition and significance. My parents screwed up methods had left me with an extreme sense of uncertainty. I'd never really felt a part of anything until now. Now, I felt important and needed. I was a significant element in the running of a household, and as a woman, I was finally vindicated. We even talked about me having a baby. Though the thought of having a baby for my wife more than excited me, there was always the memory of how she'd harshly criticized me when I was learning how to parent Angelo. Still, I was willing to take that risk. I'd even gone as far as to solicit information from several local cryogenics firms. I wanted to research our options and make the best conscious decision thoroughly. It shocked me when my wife suggested that we just pick a man and make a baby "the old -fashioned way" but I, of course, dismissed my ill feelings concerning her nonchalant attitude of the notion of me sleeping with someone else, not to mention a man. I calmly countered her idea and reiterated my wish to go through a cryobank and have artificial insemination. She seemed to be on board with my plan, though we never actually visited the clinic.

My 25th birthday was fast approaching and, though I usually had an idea of how I wanted to celebrate, I didn't have a clue about what I would do this year. B hadn't mentioned it really, and I wasn't sure if she would even acknowledge my special day. I'd never spent a birthday with her before, so I didn't know if things like that were of importance to her. I knew that her birthday was at the end of the same month and that I was going to go out of my way to make her feel special. Birthdays had always been a big deal to me, and I made sure always to put my significant other on a pedestal. I just hoped my wife would do the same.

I didn't make any plans, and when October 3rd rolled around, I nervously waited. My longtime friend, Q had come down from Lansing and showed up at the shop that day. She'd gotten her hair done and then insisted on taking me for drinks at Starter's lounge. After doing my hair and makeup, Q and I went shopping and picked out something cute to wear. She almost demanded that I wear pink and when I asked why she merely said "Do as I say Bitch! Trust me!" We both laughed as I took my pink bustier and heels to the register. We stopped by my house to change and then headed to the bar. Q was driving our usual route when she suddenly turned down Schoolcraft instead of Plymouth Rd. I didn't question her until she pulled into a parking lot that was familiar, but not our expected destination. "Why are we stopping here?" I asked.

"Just C'mon!" she demanded, almost rushing me from the car. I did as she told me and exited the car. We walked into the bar, and I was startled by a mass crowd shouting "SURPRIIIIIISE!!!" B stood at the front of the crowd with a huge smile on her face. She had on a baby blue blazer and matching hat with a pink button-down shirt, jeans, and loafers. My mother and father and all of my family and friends stood behind her greeting me. I instantly burst into tears. My wife had thought so much of me that she went out of her way to reach out to all of my family and friends to throw me this awesome surprise party. She'd spent time and money to secure a venue and plan this event just for me. I was always the one to do things like this, but I'd never had anyone show me the same love. She must as really love me to have gone to such lengths, I thought. My newfound bliss felt surreal. We enjoyed the night as we laughed it up with my family and friends. Everyone showed so much love, and I felt like a queen. We ate, drank, laughed and danced all night, and it was the best birthday I had ever had. After the party was over, B and I drove out to Novi where she had reserved a suite for us at the

Doubletree Hotel. The room was gorgeous and looked more like a high-end apartment. There was a bedroom with a huge, soft king-sized bed with crisp white linen. There were a full kitchen and a huge living and dining area. In the spacious, all marble bathroom, there was a large whirlpool tub that sat high with steps leading up to it. It was adorned with lit candles and rose petals inside. I was speechless. Never had I been pampered this way. Any doubt that I had that my wife loved me melted away. She was proving now how much I meant to her. We made love in the huge tub and the living room on the couch and floor. Then we did it on the kitchen counter before finally moving to the bed. We made love all night and then again, the next morning. B was terrific in bed. I'm sure my feelings for her were heavily fueled by how crazy our sex was. She drove me insane with her freaky, uninhibited techniques. I loved the way she ate me and even more how she nailed me to the wall every time she wore that strap.

One night during one of our sexcapades, she flipped the script on me. She had been wearing me out when she suddenly stopped. I was about to ask what was wrong when she got up and went to the bathroom. I figured maybe nature called, but when she emerged, she had taken "Mr. Magic" off and had "him" dangling in her hand like a purse. I wondered what was wrong and was about to inquire when she approached the bed.

"Here," she said, with a slight grin. I just looked at her, perplexed. She motioned again for me to take the strap from her hand.

"We done?" I asked, both confused and disappointed.

"Put it on," she said. I was stunned.

I was really under the impression that studs didn't take the strap. Every time I hinted at even fingering Angela, a heated argument ensued, so I assumed that fucking a stud was just prohibited as a cardinal rule. I couldn't believe that my wife, a stud, was offering me the chance to fuck her. Maybe this was something that she reserved just for me, her wife. I felt special, excited and nervous all at once. I loved giving strap, but this was something so new to me. I knew, still that I couldn't treat a stud and, even more importantly, my wife like the femmes I'd dealt with in the past. Nervously, I took the strap in my hands. I was filled with anxiety, but if this was what my baby wanted, I had to give it to her, and I had to make her feel comfortable. I got up and went to the bathroom. I didn't want her to see me clumsily fumbling with the complicated contraption. Once I'd secured the instrument to me, I approached my waiting wife. Slowly, I climbed on top, being sure not to move too fast. I began by kissing her softly, and then with more passion. I positioned myself and then pushed in very carefully. She was tight and gave a little resistance as I entered. I swear every time I was in pussy, I could feel it. She felt so warm, and I had to concentrate hard to keep from cumming too fast. I started very slow, being extra cautious and not wanting to hurt her. I felt her become more and more wet, as she gave less and less resistance. I began to pick up my pace a little as she began to indicate that she was into it. I leaned into her more, and we kissed passionately as I thrust in and out. She began to sound off, letting me know that I was getting warmer. I kept hitting those corners until she sang out and I knew she'd climaxed. We finished with soft, passionate kisses and we held each other as we drifted off to sleep. I thought I'd loved before but nothing I'd ever felt compared to this. I ate, slept and breathed "B."

It always seemed, however, as though the more comfortable I got, and the more I let my guard down, the more distant she would become. I'd been brainstorming ideas of how to celebrate her upcoming birthday, but I couldn't help but notice that she was staying at work later and spending less time at home. I wondered what was up, but I didn't want to rock the boat. We'd been so happy lately, and I didn't want to jeopardize that. Robert had returned home to his mother, and the house was eerily still, so it was even easier to notice my wife's frequent absence. One evening, I got off work and went to the video store to rent some movies, hoping that B and I could spend some time together. I returned home to find the house empty. It was only around five pm, so I didn't trip. I fixed a little something to eat, chilled and waited. Eight o'clock rolled around, and I began to wonder. I called B's cell phone but got her voicemail. I didn't leave a message, but I texted her immediately after. *"Hey, baby. What time are you coming home?"* It read. Another hour passed, and I received no response. *"Where are you?"* my next text read, as my anxiety turned to suspicion and then anger. Just when things seemed to be on the right track, she goes and pulls a stunt. Again! Well, I wasn't about to sit around and wait for her. I'd started to grow tired of her disregarding my feelings and what was worse was that now I felt like she owed me more respect. After all, I was now her WIFE. I hopped in the shower and changed my clothes. I called my girl CeCe to see what she had up.

"I'm chilling' girl. Come thru," she told me. I did just that, but not before stopping by the liquor store. I'd long since traded liquor in for wine, hoping to appease B, but fuck that. Tonight, I went straight for the vodka. I asked the clerk for a fifth of Three Olives. When I got to CeCe's, we went straight in on the vodka and cranberry. I was never much for vodka, but I was mad and in straight *"No fucks given"* mode. Glass after glass I knocked the vodka back. I felt the effects but not enough that I wasn't painfully aware that I still hadn't heard from my wife. My gut was telling me that she was up to no good and not just unable to call. With every moment that passed, I got angrier. My heart hurt. I was so disappointed. I thought that marriage would change her, but it was becoming clear that I had it twisted. After drinking way more than I should have, I left CeCe's and headed home. Fuming.

I don't even remember the drive home, but when I reached the driveway at around midnight, B's car still wasn't there. I exited the car and stormed into the house, only to find it again dark and empty. I was furious! Just as I reached for my cell phone to curse her ass out, I saw the headlights of the burnt orange Lexus pull into the driveway. I flung the door open and met her outside. I didn't even give her the opportunity to say anything before I was in her face.

"What the fuck?! Where the FUCK you been?!" I demanded. I didn't give her the opportunity to answer. I continued ranting and began shoving and pushing her. I was so angry and wasted that most of the dialogue was a blur, but I kept at it. She laughed it off, telling me she was at some haunted house with "co-workers." I hated her so much for making a mockery of me and our marriage. It was like she didn't feel like she owed me an explanation. She was so nonchalant and disrespectful I just wanted to rip her head off.

"I ain't got to stay here and argue with your ass! I'm out!" she declared.

She got back in her car and started it. If she thought she was going to pull off and leave me standing there, then she was sadly mistaken! I had my cell phone in my hand, and I took it and slammed it as hard as I could through the back windshield of the car. CRASH! Glass went everywhere, including in my forearm but I was too angry to feel anything.

"What the fuck?!" she yelled. "Have you lost your fucking mind, bitch!" she barked. I walked back up to her and slapped her. She tackled me. We wrestled on the front lawn and neighbors began to come out of their houses. I'm not sure how CeCe became aware of what was going on, but she pulled up in the midst of the fight. She had our friend Marvin with her, and he picked me up off my feet and pinned me to the side of the car, restraining me. I was still going crazy, arm bleeding profusely and all. CeCe had pulled B aside and tried to get her account of the story, but all I kept hearing her say was, "Get that bitch outta here!" No matter what went on, I was still her wife. How could she refer to me that way, I wondered? Even with all the fury and chaos It still hurt when she called me that. Marvin practically threw me in the back of the car and refused to let me out. I was exhausted both physically and emotionally, so I was really in no position to resist. CeCe got into the driver's seat, and we proceeded to Providence Hospital.

After having my arm treated and sleeping off much of my drunken rage, CeCe took me home with her. A lot of what took place prior was a blur, but I was reminded of what I'd done each time I looked at my heavily bandaged forearm. I tried all morning to call B, but my calls went unanswered. I started to panic. Was this the end? I know I punched the windshield out of her beloved Lexus, but wasn't I justified after she refused to come home or answer my calls? She was my wife. Didn't she owe me that? Maybe she disagreed, but that's how I felt. Still, I didn't want to break up. I wanted her to talk to me. I wanted her to come and get me, and we go home and sort this out. I tried well into the afternoon to reach her. Finally, almost approaching the evening, she answered.

"What?" she inquired flatly.

"Whatchu mean "What"?" I countered.

"What is it, Shae? What do you want?" she asked as if I was irritating her.

"I want my wife," I answered, softening my tone. "Come get me," I told her.

"I'm not coming to get you. This is not going to work," she stated. I wasn't accepting that for an answer. We were married, and I wasn't going anywhere, and neither was she.

"It IS going to work now come get me, so we can fix this!" I demanded.

"You've destroyed my car and pretty much ruined my birthday! My son is witnessing you acting crazy! I'm done!" she yelled as she hung up on me. I dialed her right back. I didn't care how many times she told me no. I was not going to let her walk away from me and our marriage. I had my flaws, but I loved her so deeply. I was good to her and good FOR her, I was convinced. Fifty phone calls later, I persuaded my wife to come and get me. I apologized and promised whatever I had to, to get her to agree. That night, she picked me up from CeCe's. We got home and made love until we fell asleep.

Chapter 35

B's birthday rolled around, and we barely celebrated. We'd been more distant than ever since the incident with her car. I'd paid to get the windshield replaced and had bought her the gifts she wanted, but nothing seemed to earn her forgiveness. I felt defeated and depressed. The arguments were nonstop these days, and she was never home. The holidays were approaching, but this house was anything but a home. We'd even stopped having sex. B had been distant before, but now she was deliberately mean. She ignored me, despite my efforts to remain close to her. I started sleeping in Angelo's room as he was usually in our room with her when he was home. I was spending time in there because I didn't want her to see me cry. I tried to continue, at least by all outward appearances. I started hanging out and drinking more to avoid the exclusion and sadness I felt at home. It had been a while, but Tayvia had even popped back into the picture. She'd had two more kids since I'd seen her and was living Taylor. We started hanging frequently, and it was a welcomed distraction. Sometimes, her cousins Kera and Clifton would come along with us. The truth was after we'd gotten emotions out of the way, Tayvia and I got along well as friends.

One evening we'd partied all- night, and I didn't get home until well after five am. I walked into the house and was headed for my hiding spot when the sound of B's voice stopped me.

"Man, fuck that bitch. I don't give a fuck about her anymore. Fuck her." She was engaged in a phone conversation, and I knew she was talking about me, but I wasn't sure to whom she was speaking. You'd think, by then, I'd be desensitized to her outrageous verbally abusive antics, but each time she spoke ill of me or called me a name, it stung. It devastated me that the woman that I loved so genuinely could have such a low opinion of me. She'd never been much for physically abusing me, but the mental scars ran deep. Sure, I wasn't perfect by any stretch of the imagination, but I was loyal. I was indeed in my feelings for her. I'd never stepped out on her or even thought of anyone else in that way since we'd been together. I literally would've laid down my life for her if I had to and that had to count for something, no matter how emotionally immature I may have been. I guess I was a glutton for punishment, as I stood there a few more moments and listened. She went on about how she didn't care what happened to me or the marriage anymore. My heart sank. I turned on my heels and went back out onto the porch. I dialed Tayvia and asked how far she had gotten.

"I'm approaching the Southfield freeway. What's wrong?" she answered.

"I need you to come back and scoop me," I said, my voice trembling from the massive lump in my throat. She agreed, and I went into the house to gather some essentials. I threw a few clothes and some personal items in a bag and went back on the porch to wait without saying a word to B. As I sat and waited in the November night air, I couldn't stop the tears from falling. How could I love someone so intensely who didn't love me? How did I end up here? How did something that started off so passionately spiral down to the catastrophe that it was today? I was dumbfounded. The thought of giving up on her never crossed my mind. There had to be a reason she was so angry. There was a reason she wouldn't let me in, and I was determined to find out why. I just needed to let things cool down and approach the situation after we'd both had a chance to calm down. Emotions were running high and we each required time to think and rationalize.

Tayvia picked me up, and we headed off to her house. On the way, I told her what I had overheard and that I felt I needed a couple of days to figure things out. I had every intention of going back home to my wife. I just had to figure out how to fix us. We couldn't go on the way we had been. We were at odds more than ever, and the tension in the air when we were around each other was thick enough to cut with a knife. We weren't happy, and I had to find a way to get us back to that happy place. I stayed at Tayvia's both Thursday and Friday. When Saturday rolled around, after work, she and I went out. I had a gig to sing at, a 50th birthday celebration, and we'd gone to another club afterward. We had a good time, and it was much needed, as I was still pretty upset about my situation. We were headed back to Tayvia's when an eerie feeling came over me.

"Red. Ride past my house. I need to see something." She did and turned down my street. When we approached the house, it was still and dark. Nothing seemed out of the ordinary except that there was an unidentified car up in the garage where I would usually be parked. I found it kind of odd, but upon closer inspection, I realized it belonged to B's co-worker. I was casually familiar with him from when I would visit her at her job. My mind eased a little.

"Do you know whose car that is?" Tayvia questioned.

"It's her co-worker. They probably fell asleep watching the game, or maybe he had too much to drink." I answered. I was satisfied that there weren't any other cars that I didn't recognize. I was just grateful that it wasn't another woman's car in the driveway. With my nerves put to rest, we headed back to Tayvia's. I still wasn't ready to head back home yet. I still hadn't come up with what to say or how to even begin to repair what was so broken.

For the next few days, I pored over what I would say to my wife when I saw her again. I wanted to tell her how much she meant to me and also how much she'd hurt me. I wanted us to get everything out on the table so that we could begin to get back on track. I wanted her to tell me what I was doing wrong and why her feelings toward me had changed. I wanted, more than anything, to be everything she wanted and to make her happy. But how could I if she wouldn't talk to me and tell me what that was?

Thanksgiving was that following Thursday, and I wanted to be in the comfort of my home with my family. I called B to tell her that I wanted to sit down and talk with her. Her response threw me off.

"I'm cooking Thanksgiving Dinner. You're welcome to come by then," she replied. I was perplexed. I can "come by?" Was I a guest now? That discouraged me. I was in no mood to be rejected by B. It hurt too much. Furthermore, I was not about to allow her the satisfaction of throwing me out of what was supposed to be OUR home. That response alone changed my whole opinion of the situation. While I wasn't ready to file for divorce, I started to realize that maybe I needed to start looking out for me since it was clear that my wife was only looking out for her. That day, I had Tayvia take me to look at an apartment.

When Thanksgiving Day arrived, I didn't feel like celebrating. I usually went to my mother's and to visit family, but I wasn't in the mood. I did go by B's as she had extended an invitation. Part of me wanted to see her and look into her eyes. I wanted to see if all hope for us was gone. I wanted to know for sure if it was over. When I got there, she and Angelo were there. Dinner had already been served, and there were a couple of guests whom I'd never met. There was one, however, that I recognized.

Her co-worker who'd been parked in my spot a few nights before was there. I spoke to him vaguely, and the weirdest feeling came over me. I blew it off and bid my goodbyes to B and Angelo. I hadn't been there long, but something didn't feel right, and I didn't want to stay. That wasn't the first time I'd felt ill at ease in what was supposed to be my house. I resumed my apartment search the very next day. I wasn't ready to fully accept that maybe my marriage was over, but I felt that I needed to secure a place of my own. I hated being at anyone's disposal, and it was clear that B was fully prepared to throw her weight around when it came to her house. I found an upper flat, not far from the salon, just up Seven Mile Road. It was only one thousand dollars to move in, and I signed the lease that same day. Tayvia had been kind enough to let me stay with her for almost two weeks. I was thankful for her kindness but, I was relieved to be in my place. The flat was small, but it would work for the time being. I didn't have any furniture, but even that didn't bother me. That would come in due time. I was just happy that I had something to call mine. I wasted no time settling in and had even gone and gotten most of my things from B's. I hadn't shared the details of my finding an apartment with her. I just went and retrieved my clothes without much of an explanation. I was still pretty upset about how she played me on Thanksgiving Day, so I felt justified in moving and not telling her.

I, also, felt like my time at Shay's had run its course. Nicara had been helpful to me, and I thanked her, but I explained that I felt the need to move on. CeCe had started working at a new salon further up Seven Mile. They'd just opened, and she said they were looking for stylists. I met with the owners, a young couple named Mike and Natalie, and they welcomed me aboard. The salon and everything in it were brand new and done with taste. Mike, whom everyone playfully called Chubby, was a nice guy. He was the big, teddy bear type and seemed to have a very gentle and laid-back personality. His fiancé', Natalie was cool, but I could tell she had a fiery side. Mike was a street nigga, turned businessman and the shop was just one of his investments. There was a restaurant that was being developed as well real estate and a strip club. They were doing well for themselves as a young couple, and I saw myself fitting into the salon nicely. I felt more at ease that I wouldn't be alone in my new environment, being that my girl CeCe worked there. CeCe was a few years older than me, and she had a wife as well. Her wife made it clear that she didn't care for me and that was just fine because I was never one to kiss ass. She made some unwarranted reference to me liking CeCe, but she was off base. CeCe and I had a purely platonic friendship, nothing more and nothing less.

About a week into settling into my new home and workspace, I arrived at the shop one morning to wait for a scheduled client. I'd been at the shop only a few minutes when the landline phone rang.

"Shae pick up line two." the receptionist signaled.

I picked up the receiver of the phone, and it was Tanya. She informed me that she tried calling my cell and a guy answered. "Did you change your number?" she questioned. I was puzzled. Then it donned on me that I hadn't heard my cell phone ring all morning, which was unusual, especially on a Friday.

"No. I still have the same number. Are you sure?" I asked.

"Yes. I called three times, and the guy got upset the third time I called," she answered. "Well come on in, Tanya. You're good. I'm going to call and see what's up." I told her. I hung up and immediately dialed my cell phone. I expected it to ring in my hand, but true to what my client said; I heard a man's voice at the other end.

"Who is this?" I questioned him.

"Who is THIS?" he retorted defensively.

"This is Shae and why are you answering MY phone?" I demanded. He abruptly hung up. I angrily dialed B from my cell phone. There was an error message recording at the other end. I hung up and called B from the salon phone.

"Hello?" she answered.

"What is going on?" I questioned.

"What do you mean?" she countered, trying to be sarcastic.

"Why the fuck is this NIGGA answering my number? I insisted.

"That's not your number anymore." she corrected.

"What?" I asked, confused.

"I gave your line away," she said flatly. I was stunned and angry.

"So, you cut your wife off, to put some random nigga on?!" I fumed.

"Are you fucking this nigga or something?" I half chuckled at my outrageous, rhetorical inquiry. There was a long pause at the other end.

"Look. I'm bringing the rest of the things you left at the house to your job," she stated before hanging up, not giving me a chance to respond. I took a break from my fury about the phone to ponder the sarcastic reference I'd made to B "fucking" this random nigga and how she'd never denied it. I was talking myself out of even entertaining something so farfetched when I thought back to that three o'clock in the morning call; her male co-worker had been so cozily parked in my parking space, and inside a dark house with my wife. It must be just the anger talking; I tried to convince myself, as I thought of how he was conveniently at my home with my wife and child having Thanksgiving dinner and the eerie feeling that made me so sick to my stomach that I had to leave.

I tried to carry on usually that day, but I couldn't shake the ill feeling that had come over me since talking to B. I was halfway engaging with my clients and not able to focus. I tried to be my witty, usual self but something was just off. I was just about done for the day when I looked up to see B at the glass door of the salon. She had bags in her hand and my vacuum cleaner that I'd left behind at the house. Was this to signify that she was indeed done with me? Even with my moving into my spot, in my mind, it was only temporary. I was convinced that one day, and soon, I would return home to my wife and family. But, somehow, with her delivering my things to me so formally, our separation seemed so final. Could her decision have any correlation to this dude all of a sudden being the deserving recipient of my cell phone line? I didn't know, but I was damn sure going to find out, I stepped behind the receptionist's desk to buzz her in. She came in and handed me the bags and immediately turned on her heels to leave.

"Hold on!" I demanded. "So, you're going to walk away without explaining yourself? Come here. Let me holler at you." I summoned sternly. She reluctantly followed me to the rear of the salon so that we could speak in private. "What is going on?" I insisted.

"Rick is my nigga," she said, flatly.

"What? Your co-worker. I know. But why did you give him my line? You know I need my phone?" I went on.

"Because he's my man." she interrupted.

"But why did you give my... Wait? What?" I stifled myself, trying to make sure I understood her correctly. I positioned myself, forcing her to look me straight in my eyes. "What you mean B?" I asked intently.

"We're a couple. She stated, flatly. Just then I felt all of the wind go out of me. My knees buckled and the wall behind me caught me. My head began to race, and I started to feel nauseous. I ducked into the ladies' room behind me and fell to my knees in front of the toilet. I threw up until there was nothing left to throw up. When I was done, I sat there on the cold floor of the bathroom feeling like some man had punched me. My whole body ached, and the tears wouldn't stop. I sat there stuck for what seemed like forever when a knock at the door startled me. I could hear, faintly, through the thick wooden door a female voice.

"Shae, are you ok? Let me in." CeCe insisted.

"I'm ok. I'm coming." I tried to say convincingly. I got up and did the best I could to look normal, washing my face and rinsing the horrible taste in my mouth. My eyes were red and puffy, but I didn't want my co-workers in my business, so I tried patting them with a warm paper towel to make it less noticeable. I emerged from the bathroom and quickly gathered my things and went outside to call a cab. Luckily for me, the car was there in no time, and I directed the driver straight to my house. I ran inside and cried myself to sleep.

I still felt weak; I didn't get much sleep at all that night. I tossed and turned and fought with crying spells until the wee hours of the next morning. I was fucked up mentally. Not only was my marriage falling apart, but my wife was carrying on another relationship with a man. I was confused and devastated. I still felt physically sick, and I couldn't stop the tears. I lay on the floor of my apartment that entire day without moving. I didn't eat, drink or even use the toilet. I just lay there, lifeless. I went on like that for two days. I still didn't have another phone yet, so

I'm sure my clients were frantic. I didn't care about anything. I just wanted to disappear.

I remember feeling like this at about twelve. My mother and I had it out, and things got heavy. She'd been on one of her drug, alcohol-fueled rants, and as usual, I was who she picked on. I'd gotten to the point, however, that I wouldn't just take her attacks lying down. I'd clap back. Though, on the one hand, it felt good to stand up for me, but it hurt on the other because it was my mother. Why couldn't she and I have the relationship and bond I'd seen my friends share with their moms? Why didn't she love and be warm like them? I hadn't witnessed their moms calling them bitches and hoes and saying hurtful things like what I endured on a regular. Well, I got tired of her making me feel like shit, and I started getting back at her with words. I was defiant and rebellious and wanted to hurt her as she hurt me. She'd called me a bitch this particular night, and I finally called her out on her drug use and told her what a sorry excuse for a mother she was. I told her I hated her, and she slapped me in the face as hard as she could. I didn't hit her back, but I kept playing that "hate" card. Later that night in my room, I cried and cried. I was so tired of her hurting me. I wondered what I could have done that I didn't deserve love from either of my parents. I tried to stop the tears, but I couldn't. I just wanted it to end. I thought maybe I was better off dead since she hated me so much anyway. She'd always treated me like such an inconvenience and put the attention of her man before me. I went to the medicine cabinet in the bathroom and got a full bottle of pills. I wasn't even sure what they were, but one by one I swallowed half of them. I lay on my bed and waited. The next day, I went to school with a splitting headache and threw up a few times, but the overdose hadn't taken the desired effect. My mother never knew it, but that would only be one of several attempts at taking the easy way out.

I managed to make it back to work after cowering in my apartment the entire weekend, but I was still very much in a daze. I went through the motions of my daily tasks but was on autopilot. I didn't feel like talking or smiling. I just wanted to get what I had to do done and go home and hide. I hid and sulked for days. Tayvia had been kind enough to put me on her cell phone plan so that I'd have a means of communication. I was grateful given the fact that my wife had double-crossed me for a nigga and my credit didn't allow me to get a contract of my own without a high deposit.

I was lying on my pallet on the floor one night, finishing off a bottle of white zinfandel, when my phone rang. It was late and not many people other than clients had my new number, so I wondered who could be calling. I read the caller I.D. and froze when I saw that it was B calling. I answered, trying to remain and sound composed.

"Hello!" "Hey baby," she countered. I pulled the phone away and stared at it. I thought to myself why she would call me baby. "I want to talk to you. I need to see you. Can I come get you?" she insisted.

Amazingly, I wanted to see her too; even with all that had happened, I needed to see her face and for her to explain herself. I hesitated, not wanting to sound as desperate as I felt.

"Yes. I do believe you owe me at least a face to face explanation." I answered. I gave her the address, and within a few minutes, she was outside. Once in the car, I was nervous. Did I want to hear my love explain to me how she'd betrayed me and, of all people, with a man? I wasn't sure I was ready for that, yet I turned to her anyway and asked. "Did you sleep with him?" There was a long and uncomfortable silence.

"Yes," she said without looking at me. Suddenly that familiar loss for air feeling engulfed me, and soon nausea followed.

"Pull over," I yelled feeling light headed. When she did, I flung open the car door and lost all the contents of my stomach. I got back into the car and tried to compose myself, but I broke down. I hated for her to see me cry but I couldn't stop the tears. She drove, and I sobbed. As emotional as I was, something in me wanted to know how and, more importantly, why. I questioned her on every detail trying to rationalize her actions somehow. There had to be an explanation as to why my wife would feel compelled to fuck a nigga in our marital bed. I wanted so much for something she said to give me some measure of understanding and comfort. How long had this been going on? Why hadn't she told me she liked men? What exactly did they do sexually? Was she going to continue to see and sleep with him? My head was swimming, and even though she was attempting to answer, much of what she said was a blur. The truth was nothing she said could comfort me. Also, her profuse apologies wouldn't take away the heaviness in my heart. The whole time we'd been together I'd been competing with her ex and now a man? How could I compete with that? I was more than devastated. I was broken.

I could barely look at B by the time she finished filling me in. I sat in the passenger seat at a loss for words. I wanted just to hide.

"Just drop me at home," I instructed solemnly. She did as I requested and as soon as we were back in front of my flat, I exited the car without saying a word. I went into the house and crawled under the covers. I laid there numb until I fell asleep. I awoke the next morning expecting to feel better, but I didn't. I still felt a sunken, heavy feeling in the pit of my stomach but, Ironically, I loved and wanted my wife. Hurt beyond words, but something in me wanted my marriage. Something in me still wanted to work things out and get past this horrible situation. I reached for my cell and saw that I had a message. It was from B, and it read: I made a mistake, but I wanted to fix it. I'm sorry. I love you. Honestly, I loved her too. I wanted her despite how she'd betrayed me. I didn't know how I would forgive her or how to get this awful mental picture dislodged from my mind, but I loved my wife, and I didn't want to be without her.

Christmas was fast approaching, and I was looking forward to spending it with B and Angelo. We'd been through a tough time lately, and I wanted to put the past behind us and enjoy our first holiday season as a family. I'd been back at the house since we talked, but I hadn't moved my things from my apartment. Part of me wanted to keep my spot just in case things went south again, but I knew if I wanted my marriage to work I'd have to give it my all. I'd decided I'd sublet once I found someone reliable and trustworthy. I had agreed to work on our marriage, with the condition that B never sees her co-worker again. She swore to me that he no longer worked at her location and that all communication had ceased. I wanted to believe her, but nowadays it was so hard to trust her. Still, I thought she was the woman for me, and I wanted my family. Christmas came, and we celebrated nicely. Angelo got all he wanted, and then some and B, and I exchanged gifts as well. Though things were outwardly going well, inside, I felt empty. Every time she was out of my sight for even the slightest amount of time, I felt anxious. I hated feeling the way I felt, and I would drink to make myself feel numb. I would drink all day at work and night when I came home. The New Year began, and I still felt stagnated and depressed. I was trying to be diligent in my marriage and my position as wife and mother, but something was amiss. I wanted so much for us to rediscover why we fell for each other, to begin with, but something in me knew she would break my heart again.

One night after work, Mike and CeCe invited me out for drinks. We went to a strip club on Plymouth where Mike frequented. He treated us, and everything was on him. That's the kind of guy Mike was. He liked to see everyone having a good time, and he didn't mind footing the bill. We ate, drank and enjoyed the beautiful entertainment. The end of the night wasted me, but that didn't stop me from hopping in B's Mitsubishi and attempting the drive home. I was riding up the icy Southfield freeway when the car started to fishtail. A black SUV slammed into me and pushed me into the median. In quick succession, another car slammed into me from behind, spinning me 360 degrees. I knew that the car was totaled, but amazingly it still drove. I knew I was in deep shit if I waited for the police, so I exited the freeway and made a beeline down Seven Mile toward the house. I made it to my driveway and attempted to get out of the car when the police confronted me. Without asking me anything, they tackled me to the ground and handcuffed me. They tossed me in the back of a squad car and carted me off to the eighth precinct. I was familiar with the God- awful place as they booked me and threw me into a cell. I was there alone for hours when I heard a female officer call my name. I got up off of the cold, hard concrete slab when she opened the cell door.

"There's someone here to see you," she informed me. She allowed me to go into the hallway, and to my surprise it was B. I was still dazed and groggy from the alcohol, but I was relieved to see her.

"Are you getting me out?" I asked, hopefully.

"I'm working on it, but they don't want to let you go for twenty-four hours. I can smell the alcohol on you still," she said, the disgust apparent in her facial expression. I paid her apparent disdain no mind. My only concern was getting out of that place.

They did make me wait the entire twenty-four hours required on a DUI before I was released. Upon being let go, B informed me that I had totaled the car. I felt terrible, but I knew that it was insured. I wasn't seriously injured, except for a friction burn from the seatbelt across my neck. They were, however, going to press charges for the DUI and the fact that I fled the scene of the accident. I enlisted the help of an attorney that CeCe knew and about $2500 and five court appearances later. The charges were finally dismissed. I had cursed the officers and refused to take any of the sobriety tests, which is what saved me ironically. The fact that I'd totaled a car and nearly killed myself didn't stop me from drinking. I still hit that bottle hard almost every day just to numb my heart and quiet my thoughts.

I'd been back and forth between my apartment and the house I shared with B since the accident. True to form, she'd started acting shady again, and this time I wasn't going to tolerate her disrespect. The truth was, I had an attitude of my own, and even I had no idea how deep-seated my anger was. When she and I would fall out, I would retreat to my private space. There was still always that unspoken suspicion that she was fucking around on me and I didn't trust her as far as I could see her. I'd bought myself another car, so I was no longer at her mercy. When she pissed me off, or I just didn't want to be bothered I could move as I pleased. My attitude toward her was different, but I never cheated. For the life of me, I couldn't understand this obligation I felt to be loyal even though I'd never been shown the same respect. I came to the house late one night after a night of drinking, and I woke B up. That familiar sick feeling had come over me, and though the alcohol-fueled my fury, my feelings were legitimate. I asked B had she been seeing her former co-worker, but I could never have prepared for her response.

"No. But I have had sex with another woman though," she said, without hesitation. I was floored. I sat there for a few minutes just stuck. That feeling of having the wind knocked out of me appeared again. I stood up and left. I drove to my apartment on autopilot and stayed the night there. The next morning, I awoke and immediately recalled the revelation from the night before. I was instantly enraged, and I decided that I wasn't going to take this sitting down. I dialed the location that B's boss worked at and informed him of what was about to transpire. I then dressed and drove to Home Depot and bought five cans of spray paint. I drove to B's house and made my mark. In bright red, I sprayed the word **"WHORE"** nice and big for the whole block to see across the front of the house. Then I got in my car and headed for her job. I saw the burnt orange Lexus parked outside the gate that surrounded the car wash and parked directly behind it. I got out, and in black, I sprayed the word **"WHORE"** on the hood, sides, and trunk of the car. I then went into the car wash and found B directing vehicles in the procession leading in.

Without hesitation, I attacked her, landing punches and slaps wherever I could. I was so livid that much of what was happening was a blur, but I punched, hit and kicked her until I got tired. When I was satisfied, I retreated to my car as the customers and co-workers looked on. I drove with no particular destination. I lit a cigarette and attempted to smoke it though I didn't even smoke. I rode around in a daze for hours until I was just tired of driving. I pulled over onto a side street and just sobbed. I wished I could get her out of my system, but I didn't know how. I wished I didn't love her. Why did I? She'd dogged me from day one just about. Did I just like being mistreated? I didn't know, but for the first time, anger and hatred started to change my perspective. I was tired of her hurting and disrespecting me, and I had to get away from her once and for all.

I wondered if it was my destiny to fall in love with the wrong woman... continually...

Publisher's Notes

Thank you for supporting the literary work of Author "Shae Mone" – with respect to the keeping the Author's voice and tone throughout this novel; we did very little structural editing.

SoZo Ink Publishing and Entertainment strives to provide writer's with a platform to display their literary talents. If you're ready to publish please submit full manuscripts to: sozoink@gmail.com.

Please check out our other published work:

"A Million Heartbreaks: Basil Jones" – by Amazon's Bestselling Author Dom LaRay bit.ly/domsbook - Published December 7, 2017

Follow us on Facebook to stay current with all upcoming events.
www.Facebook.com/sozoink

www.ingramcontent.com/pod-product-compliance
Lightning Source LLC
LaVergne TN
LVHW051501080426
835509LV00017B/1864